Developing Leaders

Through Theological Education by Extension

◆

CASE STUDIES FROM AFRICA

STEWART G. SNOOK

Developing Leaders Through Theological Education by Extension

Case Studies from Africa

© 1992 by the Billy Graham Center, Wheaton College
Printed in the United States of America

Our sincere appreciation to the following people who graciously gave permission to use the illustrations in this book: Dr. Ted Ward, Dr. Fred Holland, Phillip Turley, and Dr. Kenneth Mulholland.

ISBN 1-879089-09-2

Dedication

To Eunice
whose unfailing encouragement and love
have always inspired me

Table of Contents

List of Figures

List of Abbreviations

ACTEA	Accrediting Council for Theological Education in Africa
AEAM	Association of Evangelicals of Africa and Madagascar
AEBICAM	Association of Evangelical Bible Institutes and Colleges of Africa and Madagascar
AEC	Africa Evangelical Church
AEF	Africa Evangelical Fellowship (formerly SAGM)
AETTE	Brazilian Association of Theological Schools promoting TEE
AIC	Africa Inland Church, Kenya
AIM	Africa Inland Mission
BEATEE	Baptist Evangelical Association TEE Division, Ethiopia
BEE	Biblical Education by Extension, AIC TEE program, Kenya
BGC	Billy Graham Center, Wheaton College, Wheaton, Illinois
BTCTEE	Baptist Theological College TEE, Kenya
BTEEM	Baptist Theological Education by Extension, Malawi
BTSTEE	Baptist Theological Seminary TEE, Zimbabwe
C&MA	Christian and Missionary Alliance
CAMEO	Committee to Assist Missionary Education Overseas
CEAZ-ETD	Communaute Evangelique Alliance au Zaire Enseignement Theologique Decentralize, C&MA Decentralized TEE, Zaire
CECA-ETE	Communaute Evangelique au Centre de l'Afrique Enseignement Theologique par Extension, TEE of the Evangelical Church, Zaire

COCIN-EBS	Church of Christ in Nigeria Extension Bible School
CPKLTP	Church of the Province in Kenya Lay Training Program
EBADM	Escola Biblica da Assembleia de Deus Mozambique, Bible School of the Assemblies of God, Mozambique
EBC-TEE	Evangelical Bible College TEE Department, Zimbabwe
EBS	Extension Bible School
EBS-AEC	Extension Bible School, Africa Evangelical Church, South Africa
ECWA	Evangelical Churches of West Africa
ECWATS	ECWA Theological Seminary
ETC	Extension Theological College, Nigeria
ETD	Enseignement Theologique Decentralize, Decentralized TEE of the C&MA Church in Gabon
EWBSE	Emmanuel Wesleyan Bible School Extension, South Africa
IBE	O Instituto Biblio par Extension, Baptist Church-AEF, Mozambique
IBS	Institute of Biblical Studies, Kenya
ICM	International Christian Ministries, Kenya
KAGE	Kenya Assemblies of God Extension Bible School
MPE	Mission Protestante Evangelique (C&MA), Cote d'Ivoire
MTS	Morija Theological School, Lesotho
MYS	Mekane Yesus Seminary, Ethiopia
PAFTEE	Philippine Association for TEE
PBSE	Phumelela Bible School Extension, Alliance Church, South Africa
PEDIM	Programme d'Enseignement de l'Institute Maranatha (C&MA) TEE, Burkina Faso
q	Quotation from Questionnaire #1
SAN	Seminar Alkibab Nusantara, Indonesia
SJBES	St. John the Baptist Extension Seminary, South Africa
TAFTEE	The Association for TEE, India
TEAM	The Evangelical Alliance Mission
TEE	Theological Education by Extension
TEEAN	Theological Education by Extension Association of Nigeria
WEF	World Evangelical Fellowship

Preface

TEE is a worldwide movement of leadership training, and leadership training directly affects the ongoing life of the church in Africa. Whenever we examine growing churches we note great gaps in such training. Therefore the study of TEE is highly strategic.

I became involved in extension in 1971 when I attended a workshop in Swaziland by Fred Holland and Harold Alexander. Convinced that this was the answer to our leadership training problems, in 1972 I took part in a five-week writers workshop in Harare, Zimbabwe. At that time I began to write the first of three programmed books for the AEAM Text Project. Pastor Simon Paweh joined me in 1973 and together we began a trial run in the church with TEE. The experiment was well received, growing from 12 students to 120 in ten years.

During those years, 1973 to 1983, I led our TEE program and continued to write for the AEAM Text Project—New Testament Part I, New Testament Part II, and Hebrews. The AEAM Texts have been translated into 43 languages in Africa, plus translations for the Eskimos in Alaska, Indians of the southwestern United States, Bolivian Indians, and groups in Indonesia.

We began to network with other missions and denominational leaders through the Nguni Language Text Committee, working together to get 18 of the AEAM Texts translated into Zulu. Pastor Paweh also translated 27 texts into Southern Sutu. We taught over a dozen TEE workshops, training new leaders and helping establish new programs. Recent research has taken me into Kenya, Gabon, Nigeria, and Zaire, as well as South Africa. Since 1985 I have been director of TEAM's South African field. I have had opportunity to take a long, hard objective look at TEE and see what makes it effective—or not.

My interest in researching this topic developed out of a personal concern summed up in the following question: *Why do some TEE programs appear to succeed, while others seem to fail?* This gripping question has occupied the attention of theological educators since 1984 at the TEE conference sponsored by World Evangelical Fellowship (WEF) on Cyprus. At that time educators recognized that problems and breakdowns were occurring in some TEE programs. All felt that evaluation was due (Mulholland 1984, McKinney 1984, Ferris 1984).

My research describes TEE in Africa via questionnaires, interviews, and case studies. While I start in Africa, the principles and insights discovered have wider implications for all in theological and church education and are of importance to those in leadership development who use this complex training model. My goal is to help theological and church educators be alert to the features, trends, and problems of TEE so that they may be able to evaluate their own programs and apply the insights gained to make their TEE more effective.

This overarching purpose statement expresses my motivation to research TEE at a time when it is being tested as a viable tool for church leadership development. How do we know if TEE is functioning well and accomplishing its purpose? Christian leaders, national or missionary, who start TEE programs need to understand whether TEE can function in their situation.

Theological and church educators also need to be alert to ways TEE may became dysfunctional, so adjustments can be made for continued effectiveness through revision of their program or initiation of something new.

The object of this book is to gain practical insights into TEE as a training model, so that extension programs may be used more productively to develop the ministry of the body of Christ. I have sought to gain appropriate data to describe what is happening now with TEE in Africa to lay a basis for a discerning future.

How This Book Was Written

I have ministered in South Africa under The Evangelical Alliance Mission for twenty-eight years. Much of that time has been spent teaching in a Bible college and in theological education by extension. My years in TEE enable me to write from firsthand experience as an administrator and class leader.

Research trips to Africa and results of two questionnaires from extension programs combine to give me a perspective on and knowledge of what is happening to TEE in Africa.

Three weeks before furlough in June of 1990, I left behind the boxes, the packing, and the sorting in Johannesburg to board a plane for Nairobi, Kenya. TEE administrators from all over the continent were gathering for the All Africa Theological Educators Conference.

This was the first of my four TEE research trips sponsored by the Billy Graham Center. I travelled to Gabon and Zaire once, Nigeria twice, and Kenya three times. Valuable work was done at the All Africa Conference Workshops on TEE. The participants were enthusiastic and scholarly as they pursued solutions to problems facing TEE. While there, I distributed an open-ended questionnaire to thirty administrators as a representative sample of those who head up similar TEE programs. As a result of this questionnaire, five case studies were chosen for descriptive and comparative analysis.

On the basis of the results of the first questionnaire, a second, closed questionnaire was devised which pursued themes touching upon the internal and external factors of TEE programs. The second questionnaire was sent to all 158 programs in Africa. Seventy-eight administrators returned them to me. Considering that a few programs had several names (thereby decreasing the actual number of programs), and poor mail service (which prevented some from receiving or sending theirs), this was a good return, since 50% of the programs responded.

A student questionnaire was also devised and used in conjunction with interviews during my research trips for further background and generalizations on the conduct of TEE programs.

I personally visited each one of the five programs selected for case studies and interviewed administrators, class leaders, students, and church leaders. Additional correspondence and phone calls were used as follow-up. Each program was chosen because it represented characteristics having to do with length of time program has functioned, size, vitality, problems, and/or potential. These five case studies giving an in-depth look at specific programs are described and compared. Major components of each program are explored to determine how the program is functioning.

Rev. Dan Pochi, Steve Carley, and I drove hundreds of miles in the northeast corner of Nigeria. At each stop, I interviewed and recorded notes concerning COCIN's (Church of Christ in Nigeria) TEE program. I taped many hours of interviews with tutors, students, heads of programs, and church administrators, learning their programs from the insider's point of view.

In Gabon, I spent time with the Roland Bowmans and Julie Fehr, the coordinator of the Christian and Missionary Alliance (C&MA) TEE program. They introduced me to church and TEE leaders. The area around the church in Port Gentil where I attended a TEE class was flooded from equatorial rains—the church yard was a lake from the highway to the door. We carefully "walked the plank" together, treading over fifty yards of slippery boards to get into the church, thankful for the handrail guiding us in the dark. The enthusiasm of students, tutors, leaders, and church administrators was infectious and demonstrated the impact the TEE program was having on them and their church.

The next stop was Zaire where TEE programs are spread through six distant areas, each with a regional director. Don Dix, Tim Stabell, Laura Hickey, and Kana Mazuro Way facilitated my interviews with TEE leaders. Bill Stough helped me understand the beginnings and aim of the CECA (Communaute Evangelique au Centre de l'Afrique) program. Roads did not make travel easy—heavy trucks grind small ruts into big potholes. One truck maneuvered out of a three-foot deep pothole only to get stuck in a six-foot one down the road. Without airplane service from Africa Inland Mission and Missionary Aviation Fellowship, transport in Zaire would be very difficult and time consuming.

Flying back from Zaire to Nairobi in a six-seater Cessna, we picked our way through a large wall of clouds. The pilot skillfully maneuvered under, over, and around the storm going from 6,000 to 11,000 feet and down again. The Lord was with us through all the adventure, but I was glad to get my feet on the ground again.

In Kenya, I observed a TEE class in a young, growing church on the outskirts of Nairobi. The pastor and I wended our way through a village of tin and mud houses. Hostile looks reminded me that I was an unknown quantity to some of these people. After crossing a gully cut out by rain water, we arrived at a small church filled with wooden benches where students were gathering. Their eager enthusiasm bubbled over in testimonies of how they were applying what they learned.

Letters from administrators and interviews with class leaders gave me a firsthand source of information and enabled me to gauge the feeling of those involved. Leaders from across Africa shared the needs of their programs and sent me copies of brief histories, brochures, and catalogues describing their programs.

While in Nigeria on my fourth and final research trip to Africa, I attended an All Africa TEE Consultation led by Rev. George Foxall and sponsored by ACTEA. The well-organized papers on various facets of TEE and the recommendations for further study impressed me with the fact that extension on the continent is continuing to develop its very great potential.

The exercise of integrating material from multiple sources has given birth to this book. My personal thanks to Dr. James Kraakevik and the Billy Graham Center for the privilege of exploring "What makes TEE effective?"

Acknowledgments

If I could invent an African proverb, it would be, "a book is not written by one person!" Input comes from all directions and finds its way to the printed page. Many others helped make this book possible.

My wife, Eunice, fellow pilgrim, missionary, and friend helped me edit and clarify thoughts under the pressure of time and study. Thanks to her love and patience this book more accurately expresses what I wanted to say.

Dr. Ted Ward's Ethnography course at Trinity Evangelical Divinity School stressed observation and accurate recording of interviews, and inspired me to use the ethnographic method of research in developing my five case studies of TEE programs in Africa. Principles from his Social Science Research and Socio-anthropological Foundations courses were instrumental in forming the literature reviews in chapters two and three.

Dr. Eugene Gibbs of Wheaton Graduate School introduced me to the value of quantitative statistics such as I use in chapter five to enhance the qualitative descriptions of the case studies.

Dr. Steven C. Snook, my son, gave me some very helpful feedback on ways I could improve the statistics presentation in chapter five.

Dr. G. Dalmain Congdon, for many years my co-worker in South Africa and at one time chairman of that field, read through the manuscript carefully and offered helpful insights and suggestions.

Dr. Duane Elmer of Wheaton Graduate School interacted with me during the early stages of manuscript development.

Dr. James Plueddemann of the Wheaton Graduate School suggested a model devised by Robert Stake which helped me visualize creative ways to approach the case studies.

Dr. Lois McKinney of Trinity Evangelical Divinity School offered comments on my research question and helpful suggestions on the correlation of data.

A special word of thanks to Dotsey Welliver who carefully edited and prepared the manuscript for publication and throughout offered appreciated suggestions and encouragement.

Thanks are due also to Debbie Mott who entered the data from my questionnaire faster than a speeding bullet, and to Nikki Snyder and Tony Dawson who patiently helped me with the SSPS calculations at Wheaton College. Ginny Morris, BGC secretary, kept me supplied with the necessities to keep working and guided my first attempts at the DECmate computer.

Jane Nelson, Director of Scholarship Programs, processed my application, appointed a guidance committee, and encouraged me in the project. My advisory committee consisted of James Kraakevik,

Merrill Ewert, Eugene Gibbs, Melvin Lorentzen (whose suggestion of a twenty-five word purpose statement helped greatly), Jane Nelson, Duane Elmer, and Timothy Phillips.

A very important contribution was made by those TEE administrators, tutors and students who so willingly let me interview them on my four research trips to Africa. These are the people who gave me the "feel" for what was happening in TEE in Africa.

While it is impossible to name all those who facilitated interviews, a few should be mentioned.

Steve Carley and Dan Pochi graciously guided me in Nigeria. Special gratitude to Steve and his wife who gave me a place to lay my head. Dan and his wife and children were also models of hospitality. Other church leaders and TEE coordinators were very cordial and filled out my understanding of the Extension Bible School of COCIN.

A special debt of gratitude to Rev. Phillip Turley and his wife Phyllis who welcomed me into their home on two research trips. Phil was helpful on all counts in providing information and insight used in chapter seven. Thanks are also due him for letting me use the Urban Ministries Support Group's questionnaire in Appendix A. Others who talked with me were Dan Lowery, Rev. Manyasia, Larry Bardwell, John Mutevu, David Bouvee, Jonathan Slater, Martin Weiss, and Pastor Molehi who allowed me to observe his TEE class near Nairobi.

In South Africa, Anita Johnson, Jim Skosana, and Moses Nkosi gave me the opportunity to observe and study the Phumelela program. I observed Mrs. Johnson's class and through her cooperation was a participant-observer in a workshop on TEE. Phone interviews were also conducted from the States with other class leaders.

In Gabon, Miss Julie Fehr, Mr. and Mrs. Israel (my hosts in Libreville), Rev. Emmanuel Mamboundou, Rev. and Mrs. Roland Bowman (my hosts in Port Gentil), and Jean Bouma helped me greatly to get a picture of extension as conducted in the Alliance Church.

In Zaire, I was grateful to Rev. and Mrs. Don Dix, Rev. Kana Mazuro Way, and Rev. and Mrs. Tim Stabell who guided and facilitated my tour. Bill Stough, Sr., whom I interviewed before I took my journey, also gave me details on CECA's program.

A special word of thanks goes to those busy national and missionary administrators who filled out the questionnaires which form the basis of chapters four and five. Their thought and opinions guided much of my research.

And finally, my thanks to the board and staff of the Billy Graham Center at Wheaton College for the privilege of doing this research and especially to the director, Dr. James Kraakevik, who opened up this opportunity for me and encouraged me along the way.

CHAPTER ONE

Focus On The Problem

Problems can be opportunities or obstacles—depending on how you look at them.

TEE leaders, both missionary and national, attending the ACTEA All Africa Conference of Theological Educators in Limuru, Kenya, May 30–June 3, 1990, tackled a list of ten problems put out by David Kornfield as long ago as 1976: TEE Weaknesses (See Appendix B). Here was a group not discouraged by such a list. They had hands-on experience in the daily administration of TEE; some had organized programs from the ground up; they had faced and surmounted the difficulties of maintaining TEE programs. They had also seen first-hand the fruit of such work. The solutions propounded by these leaders were feasible, forthright, and full of vigor.

The fact that TEE has spread and become a worldwide movement should encourage all who want to see strong local church leadership. Extension is a challenging form of theological education. In the process, TEE has come up against some very big problems. Out of these problems I am motivated to engage one central issue.

Central Problem

Stated succinctly, here is our central problem: Why do some TEE programs succeed, while others fail? What reasons can be uncovered for the effectiveness of some TEE programs while others break down and collapse? Before tackling this problem, let us look at some background.

Period of Development

TEE started in 1962 as a new training model, offering the promise of developing leaders for fast growing two-thirds-world churches. It spread outward from Guatemala, becoming prominent on four continents. F. Ross Kinsler reflects on theological training and the birth of TEE in South America, Asia, Africa, and North America (1981). In *Ministry by the People* (1983) he edited a series of case studies taken from various parts of the world. The movement, first cataloged by Weld (1976, 1980), began to fulfill its promise, and church leaders were trained on a world-wide scale.

> Through TEE, thousands—perhaps hundreds of thousands—of Christians in the 'third world' have received ministry training which would otherwise have been inaccessible to them (Ferris 1990, 15).

Africa adds its testimony that leaders are being trained.

> . . . The TEE movement has made available . . . basic theological education and Christian education to enormous numbers of people who did not previously have these benefits. Many hundreds of pastors have been trained who would never have been trained by residential methods. Thousands of evangelists have received basic Bible training and many hundreds of thousands of lay Christians the same. (Hogarth, Gatimu and Barrett 1983, 146)

George Foxall lists 158 TEE programs in Africa in a mimeographed publication put out by ACTEA (1990) which gives names, addresses, sponsors, year begun, enrollment by year for the last six years, language, number of courses, and administrative/teaching staff. More schools are being uncovered with each of his questionnaires. The AEAM text project has produced thirty-five auto-didactic texts through Evangel Press, which have now been translated into forty-three African languages on a basic level. Other higher level courses are also being utilized.

Expanding Growth and Leadership Needs

Exploding church growth in Africa makes it vital that church leaders be trained. Some estimate that by the year 2000, 50% of sub-Saharan Africa will be Christian. Without appropriately trained leaders, these churches will not be able to nurture new converts or train sufficient leaders. Theological educators cannot afford to have leadership training programs stagnate or collapse in the face of great church growth.

Many Christian scholars see syncretism in the Christianity of Africa which is often mixed with traditional religion. The result of syncretism is something less than Christian. The tendency to drift toward syncretism can only be halted by effective teaching of the Word of God. We need to have solidly biblical and contextualized training. The development of biblically oriented leaders affects the degree to which syncretism will be challenged.

And yet, in the face of the rapid spread of TEE (1974-1984) and the great need for such programs to meet the challenges of our day, TEE is being questioned as a viable tool for leadership training. Some say TEE is more formal than residence schools ever were (e.g., McKinney 1981); others that TEE is losing vitality and failing in its early promise to renew theological education (Ferris 1990, 13). Are such charges justified? Or are these judgments quick and cursory, with little foundation?

Some TEE programs are effective in training church leaders. One church in the Johannesburg area had lost its pastor. The whole church was left in the hands of laypeople who had no Bible school training. At that time a TEE class of fifteen men and women leaders was beginning in the church. This group worked effectively in the church for twelve years until a new pastor came. The church not only survived, but thrived. The students led services, taught what they were learning, and gave testimonies based on their practical assignments. They witnessed to their neighbors and brought new people into the church. No loss of membership resulted. The TEE program had come to inspire members in the nick of time.

In another case, a split church recovered and began to grow again primarily through the efforts of men and women leaders who were studying through TEE. This church did have a pastor, but he had to get a job to support his family (due to the church split) and was able to function only part-time in the church. He was encouraged because the group studying TEE went house visiting and gave effective witness. They helped sustain the church through this dark period, and began several branch churches.

One of my first TEE classes consisted of only two men. Yet these men were the leaders of the church. One (a high school teacher) began to do Christian service among the young people of his church and went on to help at Scripture Union camps. He eventually left secular employment for full-time Christian work and today is the head of Scripture Union for the entire country.

Another church had four key leaders studying through TEE. Their practical work was vigorous and resulted in the establishment of a branch work, which the TEE class took on as a team project.

In another class I had a student who was the pastor of an African Independent Church. He received Christ as Savior while doing the self-study book *Following Jesus* (Selfridge 1974). He formed a class of all his church leaders, and through studying the same TEE book each one also received the Lord. They continued to study and be discipled through TEE.

On the other hand, I have observed some failures. In one situation, a small group studied for three years, yet their church activity bore little fruit. They were not making the desired impact. Why wasn't the model working? Were there mitigating factors neutralizing the expected outcomes? One class stopped because the discussion leader didn't show up. In another instance, a missionary went home on furlough; when he came back, he found the TEE program had been closed.

A program ought not to be maintained just for the sake of the program. But if that model has the potential to meet leadership training needs, it is worthwhile to find out how it works. If we as leaders discover what *is* working, and utilize insights to make our programs better, then the goals of the program will be fulfilled. If leaders of faltering programs can review and remedy these programs, desperate training needs will be met.

The Research Question

My research seeks to answer, through a descriptive analysis, the question: "Why do some TEE programs appear to succeed and others seem to fail?" Standards for effective programs are set from three sources:

1. **What the Bible declares is the pattern and result of good training, demonstrated by our Lord and the discipleship model exhorted by Paul in II Timothy 2:2.** "And what you have heard from me before many witnesses entrust to faithful men who will be able to teach others also" (RSV). Ideally TEE is suited to training leaders in a chain. Students in turn are to teach others what they learn.

2. **What theological educators and experts agree regarding an effective training program.** Training must be contextualized to the receptor culture. Both cognitive attainment and skills for service must be developed. TEE is designed to be near the context of the student and work for skills.

3. **What administrators and sponsors want from their individual programs.** The church must know what it wants a training program to accomplish. It must convey to those engaged in training, a taxonomy of its values and priorities. As a model, TEE can relate to the goals of the church in leadership training.

To ascertain how realistically TEE relates to these standards, I conducted research covering an inquiry into seventy-eight TEE programs and five case studies in Africa. To get an insider's view, I found out what extension administrators, class leaders, and students say. By interviewing church administrators, I obtained the perspective of the "stakeholders" (sponsors).

Hypotheses

1. TEE has a basis in educational theory and is a subset of adult education. The educational principles of andragogy are illustrated in TEE and are of value to those pursuing any field of theological and adult Christian education.

2. Internal factors (e.g., self-study material and discussion seminars) and external factors (e.g., the local church) are identified in the TEE model, and their interrelationships demonstrated. (These will be listed in full under *Definitions* later in this chapter.) The utilization of internal/external factors are seen and discussed by its practitioners worldwide. TEE literature frequently speaks of them. F. Ross Kinsler calls them "elements" (1981, 34–35).

3. How the component parts of TEE are handled spells the difference between a productive program and one that breaks down. Mishandling creates weaknesses which, if uncorrected, limits the effectiveness of any program. Educators risk an inferior training program for the Church if its component parts are not used correctly.

Delimitations

My research deals with only one model of theological training: Theological Education by Extension. It does not deal with other forms of formal or nonformal education (e.g., correspondence courses). Nor will an attempt be made to discuss the merits of residence versus extension training. Both are learning to live together, and both have gained mutually helpful insights from each other for more effective training. Where real change is desired, effective programs can be designed in all types of training (Ferris 1990).

No attempt will be made to describe programs outside of Africa. Case studies and questionnaire results, however, may strike a responsive chord in readers all over the world who use (or contemplate using) TEE or some of its methodology.

The design of this study is descriptive and comparative, with a basis laid for an evaluative model. Description necessarily precedes evaluation and is differentiated from it (Stake 1967).

Definitions

Theological Education by Extension

TEE is a field-based form of theological education which does not extract the student from his normal, productive environment (Winter 1978). Theological training comes to the student in his home area in a decentralized fashion.

Mulholland (1976, 66) delineates similar parameters in a definition of TEE. "It is a field based approach which does not interrupt the learner's productive relationship to society." In the words of Kinsler, "TEE extends the resources of theological education to the functioning and developing leaders of congregations" (1981, 31).

TEE is theological in the sense that the content, motives, and skills derived from the Bible and theology are central. The focus is particularly on pastoral theology; students do the work of the ministry.

TEE is education in that it aims to change students in attitude and knowledge and develop their skills.

TEE is extension in that it brings training programs within the reach of people where they live. "We must take our training programs to the local church, because they cannot come to our seminaries and institutions" (Kinsler 1981, 31).

TEE Program

A TEE program actualizes the model in an attempt to develop church leaders, whether pastoral or lay. TEE programs have often been called schools, accentuating their formal nature and their ties with academic institutions. But while grades and certificates may be given, TEE programs in Africa are not usually schools in the formal sense. The word "program" is broader and allows for nonformal orientations which meet the needs of local churches.

TEE Model

The founders of TEE set out on a new and revolutionary course. They were dealing in innovative ways with the problems of leadership training. In the first eleven years of TEE's existence, which I call the period of origination, those involved were not always agreed on how this decentralized training should be conducted. There were no guidelines. They were doing something new. A synthesis of essential ideas emerged from this period leading to a new model.

The initiation of the TEE model has been traced from its inception by Ralph D. Winter, James Emery, and F. Ross Kinsler in 1963 up to the development of the split-rail fence model by Ted Ward in 1972. The fence model defines the original design of TEE as three-fold: self-study materials, the service of the student, and discussion seminars (Ward and Rowen 1972)

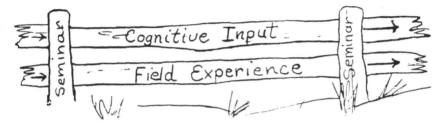

Figure 1. Fencepost Analogy

Learning centers were near students' homes. Reading, writing, and practical homework assignments were given. Students gathered periodically for a discussion class.

Restated, three educational components were put together in the original design of the TEE model:

1. Cognitive input utilizing self-study material.
2. The experience of the student-participant serving God.
3. Reflection on one's action in group discussion.

Praxis Oriented Program

A praxis oriented program is one in which the interaction of the three essential component parts function in a reflection-action-reflection pattern. The first component part (self-study material) involves reflection. Students reflect cognitively on a biblical lesson. The second component part (service to God) involves action—the participants act in response to their previous reflection. In the third component part (group discussion), they bring the results of their service to the discussion seminar and reflect on the consequences of action to refine and better their ministry.

Component Parts

The component parts of TEE are the seven elements or ingredients which constitute the internal factors discussed in this book. They are comprised of the three praxis elements: self-study materials, discussion seminars and the service of the student; and four others which directly affect TEE: administration, the type of student, the seminar leader, and a spiritual base for the program. These component parts are internal or intrinsic to the model and programs. As we examine the phenomena of TEE programs in Africa where distance and isolation breed distinctives, we may discover other component parts integral to a functional program.

Internal Factors

Without the internal factors listed and defined below, the TEE model is not complete.

1. *Type of Student.* TEE requires participants drawn from the natural leaders in the church; mature, spiritual, and accepted by their peers. The terms "student" and "participant" are used interchangeably.

2. *Self-study* materials. These are home study materials which may be written, pictorial, or oral in nature (e.g., cassette tapes). The self-study material provides cognitive input for the student away from the seminar setting. Ideally, self-study materials are a springboard for an integrated learning experience in the subsequent discussion group.

3. *Service* in the church. Participants are expected to be involved in a local church-based ministry. Evangelism, discipleship ministries, and pastoral work are common means of service. Their daily experiences become the grist of the learning mill. As they share these experiences, reflection has its fruit in application, and application in service.

4. *Discussion Seminars.* The discussion seminar consists of a small group (three to fifteen participants) interacting over their lessons. The seminar is designed for reflective interaction in which cognitive input and experiential learning are integrated. Affective change in the lives of the students takes place here.

Learning in groups is generally recognized as the most effective means for bringing about change in attitudes and behavior ... the social support stimulates thinking, and the sifting of ideas in social interaction serves as an error-correcting mechanism. (Mezirow 1972, 1)

5. The Discussion Group *Leader* (monitor, tutor). This individual represents the key personal element. The leader in TEE catalyzes the group into discussion. A trained leader guides the students in dialogical thinking, vital to problem solving.

6. *Spiritual Foundation*. A spiritual base underlies the other component parts of TEE. This category posits a whole new dimension. It represents the fact that the Holy Spirit is active in, motivating and challenging the whole church. Leadership training must be grounded in realities designed for spiritual formation. There has to be a spiritual base expressed in a purpose statement with spiritual formation as the goal (Holland 1983, 105, 106). Without spirituality as the goal, a leadership training program is sterile.

7. *Administrative Supervision*. Administration of TEE focuses on the faithful care for and oversight of the details of the program. Administrative leaders facilitate the program. The necessity for an alert administrator of TEE is an increasingly important dynamic. For the program to remain workable, the administration must be creative in obtaining materials, organizing classes, keeping records, and training tutors.

These seven factors are examined in case studies as part of the descriptive process by which effectiveness can be measured.

External Factors

External factors are in essence relationships to groups outside the program. Relational groups are the local church, the community, church administrators, and academic institutions. It is essential that TEE maintains good relationships, because learning takes place in a network of such relationships.

1. *A local church*. TEE was designed with the local church in mind. Participants are trained in the church context and actively related to a body of believers. Much of student service is carried on in the local church.

2. *The community*. The student is not in isolation. He is part of a community with a whole range of needs. Wherever the student lives is a place of ministry. TEE provides education to the participant for immediate application in the community in some practical-help stance:

evangelism, health, social aid, or other action related to broad life concerns.

3. *Church Administrators.* These are top level church leaders who administer the denomination nationally or regionally. They relate to the TEE program as sponsors and stakeholders; i.e., having a stake in the results which accrue from it.

4. *Academic institutions.* A TEE program is sometimes linked with a residence school or larger academic community which sets standards and may attempt accreditation. TEE students may enter such institutions for further training and receive credit for the work which they have done in TEE. A church program without formal accreditation from existing schools is defined as nonformal. Official grades and diplomas for credit are not the essential concern; they may be (and often are) given.

Intangibles

1. *Enthusiasm of the leaders.* Whether we look at TEE class leaders or administrators, the immeasurable quality of enthusiasm is an index of strength. TEE is about people. That desire or eagerness to move a program forward stands as the first intangible.

2. *Motivation* of the students. The underlying reasons for students remaining and working to some purpose in a program is difficult to measure. Nevertheless, motivation appears as a factor in my research because the effectiveness of the program is tied up with the motivation of those studying. When TEE first began it was dealing with highly motivated participants, which gave it its ethos.

3. *Meeting of felt needs.* A church may have many felt needs; primary to TEE are a felt need for Bible instruction and a (real as well as) felt need for leadership development. When the natural leaders in the church are being developed through study of the Word in TEE, the felt needs of that church are being met. In this we stand face to face with another intangible not easily seen on the surface. For instance, if leadership is viewed as an ordained and visible clergy, it may hinder perception of true leadership development within the church.

4. *Blessings.* How do you measure a blessing? Some blessings are tangible-numbers of students, graduates, and tutors trained. There are also those which are less tangible, and to which I refer here— a changed life, development of spirituality, and progress testified to by students. These things are observable yet immeasurable.

The definitions listed in this chapter are referred to throughout the book and touched upon in each case study.

The following chapter uncovers through a literature review how TEE reflects adult educational principles.

Chapter Two

How TEE Reflects Educational Principles

TEE is a form of adult education. The principles which educators everywhere have found to be effective in adult learning are the very ones embodied in the methods used in the TEE model.

Four major research traditions emerge as particularly relevant: adult education (andragogy) and continuing education (two streams which I combine), nonformal education, and distance education. Each of these streams has principles of learning reflected in TEE. Methods derived from these four educational traditions give the model its shape.

Adult and Continuing Education

Malcolm S. Knowles calls adult education andragogy. In his definitive work, *The Modern Practice of Adult Education* (1980), he outlines a philosophy of how adults learn (37–54). Adults are:

1. self-directed
2. rich in experience
3. concerned with personal development
4. problem-focused
5. concerned with direct application of learning

We will examine each of these in turn.

Self-Direction/Motivation

The first key statement is that adults as learners are *self-directed*. Adults *choose* to study; it is not compulsory. When adults decide to participate in an educational experience, they are saying that it is *worthwhile* to study. Stephen D. Brookfield presents a broad spectrum of issues in his book (1987). His key distinguishing characteristic between pedagogy and andragogy is that adults have autonomy of direction.

Jerome Bruner (1966) emphasizes the theory that learning takes place when it is prompted by the learner's own motivations. Learners do best when they are relatively free from the influence of external rewards and punishment (Srinivasan 1977, 11). Learning is its own reward. Joyce and Weil (1986) stress that it is the student who does the learning and that he or she is the most powerful person in the teaching/learning situation.

His or her intelligence, adaptability, creativity, motivation, and general configurations of personality are much more important determiners of how much he or she will learn than anything the teacher or curricula system can do. (404)

TEE capitalizes on the participant's own motivations as an adult learner in the spiritual realm.

When Pastor Simon Paweh and I opened our first TEE classes in 1973, church leaders adopted the goals of TEE as a tool to develop leadership in the church, increase Bible knowledge, teach scriptural ways to handle problems, and bring spiritual and personal growth. They chose to begin TEE in their churches.

Rosenblum (1985) states that if adults help plan their educational experiences, they will be more concerned, interested, and committed to the educational process (18). To give them choices is to treat them as adult learners, not children. Nevertheless when adults come into a learning environment, they often assume a dependent stance. This seems to be especially true for many adults in Africa. Educators of adults need to deliberately plan for participation in decision making and cooperative action in the learning environment. This lifts the learner back into the adult mode. "The full participation view of continuing education supports the view that planning for adult learners should not be done unilaterally by the teacher-expert" (Rosenblum 1985, 17).

TEE planners could not at first give participants much choice in regard to courses. They took what was available. Within that structure, however, felt needs were expressed; from time to time participants voiced what they needed and wanted in the way of further instruction on the subjects they were learning. TEE allows for this kind of latitude. Extra material can be incorporated into any study as the problem-solving adult learner makes the need known.

For example, in a class I held in Sasolburg (in the Orange Free State, South Africa) the students had a felt need for instruction on sermon preparation. They had been asked in their self-study books to prepare sermons but had little prerequisite instruction on how to do it. As they discussed their struggles with the assignment, right there in the class we began a session on sermon preparation. On a blackboard made by the students, important steps for sermon-making were outlined.

This "diversion" was appropriate to their learning experience; it fit in with the demands of the curriculum to prepare a sermon. It was instigated by the felt needs of the adult learners themselves. The blackboard exercise led into several more discussion classes on how to build the skill of crafting a sermon. Five in the class are still using these skills today, and one has become a full-time pastor back in the mountains of Qwa-Qwa, on the border of Lesotho. They knew what they needed to learn and were given opportunity to influence the curriculum in that direction.

Experience of the Learner

The second characteristic we build on is that adults are *rich in experience* (Knowles 1980, 37–54). The educator of adults builds the experiences of his students into the learning process. In essence, the student's experience base (informal learning) creates the context for rich encounters with new material, opening the way for new experiences.

The great educator John Dewey said, ". . . the central problem of an education based upon experience is to select the kind of present experiences that live fruitfully and creatively in subsequent experiences" (1937, 16–17).

Paulo Freire (1990b) says that political and educational plans fail because authors designed them from their own point of view, "never once taking into account . . . the *men-in-a-situation* to whom their program was ostensibly directed" (83). Since all learning is experience centered, experience must be reckoned with in TEE.

Phyllis Cunningham in her article, "Extracting Meaning from Experience" (1983), gives new meaning to a favorite saying of my father, "You live and learn." Adult learners cannot divorce their learning from their experience. Educators, therefore, need to know how to utilize experiences in learning situations to facilitate collaborative, self-directed, and community education (59). Again and again the Gospels show us how Jesus helped the disciples integrate God's

Word with their experience. The central feature in the design of TEE is to integrate personal experience and biblical learning. Two primary concerns with experiential education are assessment and legitimization. Assessment is of importance because learning from prior experience is substituted for traditional classroom hours. Legitimization has to do with official credit given for experience. One of the problems TEE faces is accreditation given for experience in serving the Lord. Accreditation must be considered for functionality, not just academic equivalence. Ferris points out that ministry experience must be allowed to dictate the limits of curriculum scope and thereby effect accreditation (Ferris 1982, 308). The whole issue of equivalency must be geared to servant leadership.

TEE seizes upon the experiences of the student and not only informs but reforms in the process of biblical study and peer group interaction. The weekly discussion group brings biblical information alongside experience so that the student can reflect and interpret experience. By expanding the information base via experiences and application of the Word, the student grows.

Educationalists speak of the action-reflection-action praxis (Groome 1980, 154). God uses praxis to teach us. The Holy Spirit takes the truth of God and helps us apply it to our lives. "Dynamic adult education has necessarily to be linked with the conditions and reality of the life of the learner" (Mehta 1978, 40).

Personal Development

A third characteristic of andragogy is that we as adults are concerned with *personal development* (Knowles 1980, 37–54). We want to accomplish something. Adults begin to have new goals, especially in middle age. At these "teachable moments" adults are wide open to new ideas and possibilities. When we see a "teaching situation" arise and combine it with an obvious "want to learn" recipient, we have the best learning environment.

Bruner says that instruction is, after all, an effort to assist or shape growth (1966, 1). He lists six points to define growth—increasing independence, internalizing truth, ability to state intention, ability to interact with others, ability to use one's language, and the ability to deal with alternative solutions and consequences (5–6). "The heart of the educational process consists of ... translating experience into more powerful systems of notation and ordering" (21). TEE helps the learner to "order his steps by the Word of God."

Personal development involves initiative, resourcefulness, and needed skills. We "cannot view process and content of adult education in isolation from the general development activities of adults" (Mehta 1978, 36). Mehta presents a chart which shows how the overlap of learning and total life situations leads to great value for the participant (39). He says, "Dynamic adult education has necessarily to be linked with the conditions and reality of the life of the learner" (1978, 40). Spiritual development in the real world is the aim of TEE and part of its base.

Apps (1979) says that adult education is concerned with people, their growth and learning. He views human beings as having qualities which set them apart. They have a dynamic internal world of meaning. Time, symbols, emotions and social dimensions distinguish persons from higher animals. The adult is more than a mature child, more than just above eighteen years old. The adult is consciously aware that education will benefit personal development and growth. It may lead to greater proficiency in the chosen field, or to a career change.

The willingness of an adult learner is hard to gauge, but certain things are obvious. If students keep showing up and sharing how they are using material learned, something good is happening. In an urban-rural survey used in Kenya on why students value TEE, 84% said they value TEE because they *use* what they learn in class (Urbanization 1990, 5).

Problem Solving

Knowles' fourth point is that adults are *problem-focused* in their learning (1980, 37–54). They have been wrestling with real problems in the real world. They want to see problems solved. Adults learn more when problem solving. It becomes the highest form of learning. Problem solving shows whether or not the student has really comprehended, because all of his resources are tested.

In problem solving, the learners decide what problems they would like to work on. Problems and their solutions are unique. By helping others solve their problems, new insight can be gained for one's own. If an instructor knows that students have acquired the rules or experience to solve a problem, problem solving can be facilitated (Joyce and Weil 1986, 429). "Certainly, one of the goals of education is to help individuals work effectively together in finding better solutions to problems they face, whether at work or home" (Mouton and Blake 1984, 176).

Adult learning *must be problem and experience centered*. Bruner summarizes learning and problem solving by saying, "If information is to be used effectively, it must be translated into the learner's way of attempting to solve a problem" (1966, 53).

Underlying the aims of experiential learning is the matter of empowering the underprivileged. In two-thirds-world countries, it is often the poor or underprivileged who are studying. It gives them the opportunity to think, solve their problems, and shape their world. They become aware that they are children of God, that this is His world, and that they can make a difference. Transformation of the social process for survival and well being are in view (Cunningham 1983, 63). "Learning and knowledge cannot be discussed intelligently outside the existence of social relations" (68).

The TEE discussion seminar is intended to be a forum for problem solving. The lesson is discussed and applied; the problems arising out of this process help the students think in new ways to solve problems, both in life and in the church. Not only is proven adult educational theory vindicated, but participants remain interested because they are seeing something changed in their lives. For example, 94% of students in an urban-rural survey said that *studying through TEE improved their family life* (Urbanization 1990, 6).

At the end of the year, a student in one of my TEE classes gave this testimony. She had many problems in her home, and little control of the circumstances surrounding most of the difficulties. However, while studying *Looking at the Old Testament, Part I* (Dominy 1974), she became aware of the manner of life adopted by Moses—"he was faithful in all his house." This woman decided that while she could not change other people or circumstances, she could incorporate this into her own life: whatever part lay with her, in whatever she was responsible for, she, like Moses, could be faithful.

After many months of carrying this out, she told us in the discussion class that most of the situations had become distinctly better, and a few were no longer problems at all. She had been able to deal with real problems in her very real world.

Direct Application

Andragogy further teaches us that adults are concerned with the *direct application* of learning (Knowles 1980, 37-54). They do not learn in a vacuum. They are surrounded by experiences and relationships. When they are able to put something to use immediately, that learning experience stays with them. The first time one gets a flat tire is the time for application. With tools in hand, the adult directly applies what he has learned in a real situation. True training is the "systematic development of the attitudes, knowledge, and skill patterns required by an individual in order to perform adequately a specific task" (Draper 1989, 86).

Knowles' emphasis on experience and application is represented by the bottom rail of the fence in the TEE model—Christian service, a vital component in the learning process. Each subsequent class gives opportunity for feedback and discussion on the experiences in Christian service that week. Every new insight gained can be applied immediately. What the adult student did and how it worked out become important discussion matters.

I gave an assignment to my Daveyton TEE class on *Bringing People to Jesus* (Moyo and Holland 1973), a course on evangelism. They were to relate the verses on salvation, which the class had just memorized, to someone they thought did not know the way of salvation. What these students did, and how it worked out, became the center of some exciting discussion.

In the first episode one lady led the witchdoctor in her home community to the Lord by sharing salvation verses. Follow-up was discussed, and in subsequent weeks she told us the new convert asked such questions as, "Shall I burn my witchdoctor's paraphernalia?" The TEE students were guided in their response by their TEE class, where they were now studying the burning of magic books and artifacts in Ephesus (Acts 19). The student was able to apply this directly to the situation of her converted witchdoctor; a bonfire was made and the tools of witchdoctoring publicly burnt. The episode has been a lasting testimony in Daveyton.

This example of action-reflection-action was enhanced by the input of the Word. Actions became biblically informed, testimony was strengthened, and best of all, the kingdom of darkness lost a practitioner.

Nonformal Education

The second major research tradition relevant to andragogy is nonformal education. It is distinct from the formal education of school and the informal unstructured learning of daily life and consists of short-term specialized instruction for utilitarian purposes. For example, a producer of agricultural products will gather farmers in an area for instruction on how to use them to best advantage. A church may gather its people for seminars on evangelism explosion. This is nonformal education.

Ward and Dettoni (1973) state that "nonformal education starts with the felt needs of people and helps them achieve their goals" (25). In 1974, Russell Kleis put together reports of over 40 studies of nonformal educative programs. They range from humanity studies of a university in Africa to health and agricultural programs in many places in the world. His report (1974) defines nonformal education (NFE) as any intentional and systematic enterprise in which content and media are selected and adapted for particular students to maximize attainment of the learning mission (8). TEE's nonformal nature is revealed when we consider that it touches upon a select group of leaders to attain a certain mission.

Kleis notes that five components must be in place to make a nonformal program viable (7–8, 312ff). These are:

1. sponsors—who support it
2. mission—the goals or target of the activity
3. content—the subject or message
4. clientele—participants who will be the students
5. agencies or media—how the instruction will be transacted

Obstacles to Nonformal Education

Ward and Dettoni's article (1973) also points out difficulties associated with nonformal education. The first obstacle is the serious and difficult groundwork of cultural and subcultural analysis (28). There are hard questions to ask related to cultural values and how nonformal programs fit into these values. An adequate diagnosis of the situation of a given community is needed before an indigenous instructional system can be developed. I sometimes wonder if enough of this kind of spade work is being done before local TEE programs are launched.

Another obstacle to nonformal education is psychological resistance to innovation and reluctance to take risks (Srinivasan 1977, 28). When traditional and formal patterns of schooling brought by colonial systems were adopted as the accepted mode of education by indigenous peoples, later acceptance of other less traditional modes was hindered. For example, in New Guinea church leaders do not have much success with nonformal education (Bray 1984, 48) because colonial types of education are heavily entrenched. In Africa, the French and English educational systems emphasize the lecture method and a philosophy which stresses pouring knowledge into heads like empty vessels. By contrast, the Kenyan urban-rural survey revealed 72% of TEE students *disagree* with the statement, "I learn better when the teacher lectures" (Urbanization 1990, 5).

Orientation of Nonformal Education

Nonformal education focuses on practical, functional, and often, work- and job-related education as a response to a 'now' situation (Ward and Dettoni 1973, 18, 24). TEE is certainly a nonformal type of education in this sense. The 'now' situation for the church lies in the areas of leadership training. Development of skills and of leadership represent two of their felt needs.

The whole idea of voluntary associations, such as the church sponsorship of NFE activities, is exemplified in many secular endeavors (Kleis 1974, 279ff). TEE can function in a nonformal setting sponsored by the church as a volunteer society. NFE includes what is referred to as "extension" education, where educational resources and skills are placed within the reach of willing participants. Extension is strong when it finds out the needs of participants, welcomes the planning and insights of learners, and casts the educative content in terms of their world view.

Paulo Freire attacks extension training if it means superiority of the teacher, transmission of content mechanically, without dialogue with the recipients of the "messianic" knowledge (1990a, 93–101). Freire overdraws his argument to make a point that any form of education can be oppressive and dominating if it does not view people as equal in worth, dignity, and thinking capability. By setting out a negative definition of extension, Freire begs the question in his otherwise insightful treatment. Extension does not imply domination; it implies sharing in context.

"Extension is extending (placing within the reach of natural leaders of our churches) the resources of theological education" (Kinsler 1981, 25). The word "extension" means making something available, not imposing courses, which are in fact voluntarily applied for.

The Word of God forms the central resource material for learner-teachers in TEE. TEE offers a body of content and also gives disciples opportunity to discuss application. Extension demands more than a transference. It includes dialogue in which contextualization becomes reality. Recipients become directive, indicating how and where the content can be applied. Conscientization occurs in the praxis of

extension as learners become aware of their environment. Both giver
and receiver reach out and talk about what they are learning and how
it can best be applied.

Distance Education

The third major research tradition, distance education, implies the
absence of the physical presence of a teacher (or that the teacher is
present only on occasion). It involves preproduced courses, a wide
range of media, and mass production of educational materials (Kaye
1985, 3, 1433). It also involves two-way communication with planned
and explicit catering for individual study. Distance education is a
"guided form of didactic conversation" (3, 1432).

Design

More precisely, distance education promotes learning wherein
the student, separated from the teacher, joins contractually in a
teacher-learner continuum. The student is assessed, given guidance,
and prepared for examinations. Learning may be individual or in
groups (Conner 1989, 23).

Distance education is included in our study because it is dependent on self-instructional material. Self-instructional material, one of
the component parts utilized by TEE, is carefully designed for use
between the visits of the tutor. Distance education and TEE also use
similar principles in the writing of this instructional material.

Course developers have the tremendous job of estimating the
needs of their target student. They write a mediated course

> to arouse attention and motivate; to link up with previous
> knowledge and interest; to present the material to be learned;
> to guide and structure, offering guidance for learning; to
> activate; to provide feedback; to promote transfer (of learn-
> ing); and to facilitate retention. (Holmberg 1979, 23)

The formidable task above is nothing compared to preparing
courses for *intercultural* distance education.

Distance education used to be a private, print-based form of study
associated with correspondence courses. Now it is defined as
noncontiguous communication with some form of two-way communication between teacher and student. All kinds of technology mediate
the instruction, not only paper (Garrison and Shale 1987, 12–13). But

"the distinguishing feature of distance education is a means of extending access to education to those who might otherwise be excluded from an educational experience." (10–11). TEE parallels this feature.

Objections

The lack of face-to-face interaction with the teacher or group calls into question the value of distance education. "If you have the technology without face-to-face groups, in educational terms, nothing much will happen" (Young 1978, 78). Sometimes, therefore, distance education has reintroduced live teachers, as in the British International Extension College (73).

Another criticism of distance education has been that it depends on rote learning. But according to Conner, "the way in which the system is organized and the courses designed will determine whether rote learning is encouraged or not" (1989, 8). He goes on to claim that distance education holds no more of a 'corner' on the rote learning 'market' than conventional education (1989, 8). I have heard the same criticism of the AEAM programmed instruction materials for TEE and reiterate the same disclaimer as Conner.

Wedemeyer cautions those contemplating a distance educational system to specify the strategies of the didactic process. "Equally it is vital to clarify the strategies which will be used and ensure that the ways and means adopted are sufficiently robust to enable agreed upon goals and objectives to be achieved" (1981, 101). Careful planning for and a biblical understanding of TEE precludes premature failure of TEE programs. Time must be taken in the beginning to assess needs, seek understanding with leaders, and plan for the long term. Programs suffer from a whole spectrum of ills related to lack of planning.

Students in distance education do not get immediate and personal feedback unless their texts are heavily programmed. Conner comments that "Frequent communication and feedback via correspondence, phone calls, and computerized bulletin board can do much to eliminate a student's sense of isolation" (1989, 18). Such contacts are not as personal as a weekly meeting with the teacher. Africa is a culture which demands personal contact.

Borje Holmberg, a pioneer in distance education, views all accessories to it as help for the individual learner (1979, 18-30). His philosophy is that learning is an individual matter. Many would debate with Holmberg on this issue saying people learn even better in groups (cf. Mouton and Blake 1984). The rationale for group learning is clear in African society where social orientation favors group living.

Holmberg emphasizes that there is "a kind of guided didactic conversation" which goes on between the instructor (in the written or oral media) and the student. The conversation is both real and simulated (1979, 20). Holmberg also says that learning may be an internal conversation with oneself or an interaction with a formal representation of knowledge designed to facilitate understanding. The term, "surrogate tutor," is used. Even though Perraton also claims that "it is possible to organize distance teaching in such a way that there is dialogue" (Sewart, Keegan and Holmberg 1983, 39), many doubt that it equals face-to-face learning.

An interesting twist is the claim that tutors have an adverse effect on the learning process and that it is actually a drawback to have one around. "Efficient tutors . . . are apt to take command and teach instead of guiding or advising, thereby depriving the students of initiative and taking over part of the function of the self-instructional course" (Holmberg 1979, 25). Chapter five reveals what is happening on the tutor level in African TEE.

Conner claims that group interaction and the possibility of discussion are inherent aspects of distance education (1989, 9). He cites Perraton, an authority on distance education, as saying that the use of tutors encourages critical reflection and promotes dialogue as an integral part of many programs (9). In any case, the necessity of feedback, interpersonal contact with the teacher, and group work are now being included as natural components of distance education.

Distance education is often wedded with "open education" where multiple media are involved. The key is the "degree of integration achieved" for greatest effectiveness (McKenzie, Postgate and Scupham 1975, 338). Courses must be planned with great care, and cooperation with radio and television must be cultivated.

TEE connects with distance education in its development of self-instructional materials. In Africa, the TEXT project has already produced 35 programmed texts. Besides the programming itself, authors were urged to make the text a "guided didactic conversation." Nevertheless the oft unbroken text (except for space for answers) has discouraged slow readers. The absence of pictures and diagrams in some books keeps them from being as interesting as they could be. Gagne states clearly that

Pictures add many valuable features to instructional events, when employed in combination with either printed or oral communications. Their function in supporting encoding and retrieval functions is considered critical. (1965, 312)

Planning

A formula for planning comes from Kaye and Rumble (1981, 23): when faced with the decision whether or not to use a form of distance or extension education, ask a series of elimination questions. Begin by defining needs.

Ask: is there an existing system to meet the need?
>   If yes, go no further in planning.
>   If no, investigate an alternative to meet the needs.

Ask: is distance education a viable solution?
>   If no, go no further.
>   If yes, decide on level of course complexity and preferred
>   form. Consider implications of cost and manpower.

Ask: is the form a viable solution?
>   If no, go no further in planning.
>   If yes, start planning for implementation.

Using TEE in leadership training situations demands the same thorough and rigorous planning strategy.

Conclusion

The commonality of needs, problems, and principles which are discovered in each of the educational approaches of adult, continuing, nonformal, and distance education gives us a valuable data base for application to TEE. Lessons learned from these disciplines help us avoid many pitfalls as we not only see parallels but carefully apply them.

I turn now to a review of the literature of the Theological Education by Extension movement, revealing its underlying philosophy, design, and problems.

CHAPTER THREE

How TEE Developed

Historical Development

Before analyzing the results of questionnaires (chapters four and five) and examining representative programs (chapters six through ten), the theoretical foundations of TEE as a leadership training model need to be set forth. My historical outline of TEE development sets the general framework of this chapter:

Date	Period
1963-1974	Period of Origination
1975-1984	Period of Rapid Expansion
1984-Present	Period of Evaluation

1. Period of Origination—Plans for a new approach to theological education were begun in 1962 and 1963 (the usual date given). By 1974, Ward's split-rail fence model was in general use (Ward and Rowen 1972, 17–27).

2. Period of Rapid Expansion—TEE spread quickly. Not only was there a soaring number of programs (Weld 1980), but a wide geographic spread in many countries on four continents. Kinsler draws twenty-eight cases from programs all over the world (1983).

3. Period of Evaluation—Since the publication of the book, *Cyprus, TEE Come of Age* (1984) in which Mulholland gives an assessment of its first two decades (9–25), TEE entered an era of evaluation and revision. The impact of TEE is now being assessed. Formative evaluation is taking place. Hogarth, Gatimo and Barrett state, "To be fair, we are only just entering the phase when the phenomenon's character can be judged as movement or mission" (1983, 147).

Component Parts of Classic TEE

Many programs today that are *called* TEE do not possess the primary characteristics of classic TEE. I referred to these characteristics as component parts in chapter one. As Patricia Harrison (1990, 27) says,

> I use TEE to indicate that type of distance theological education which combines *home study materials* and *practical ministry* experience with regular *seminars* in which tutors and students can interact. In TEE proper, the weight of the cognitive input is carried by the home study materials; it is not given in lectures. The seminars provide opportunity for interaction and for learning experiences which cannot readily be obtained through home study [italics mine].

A basic understanding of TEE assumes at least these three component parts: self-study books for individualized study; practical service by the students in their local church; and the "marriage" of these two by a group seminar, held regularly, and designed to integrate knowledge and experience in the life of the student.

When Coca-Cola changed its formula, a large outcry resulted. People wanted classic Coke. Notwithstanding new, diet, and caffeine-free Coke, some liked the old taste better. Coca-Cola was smart. It produced all kinds, even though they are quite similar.

Robert Ferris asks if TEE is still TEE even when there are no self-study materials. He says that TEE is more of a vision or movement of leadership training in context rather than a set of materials in a certain training model. He advocates looking at TEE as a vision for leadership using any method which reaches the people in a geographical area with minimal cultural dislocation (1978, 3). This may be new Coke to some, but it's still Coke.

Lois McKinney defines TEE as "the contextual, experiential development of servant leaders by, for and within the church" (1984b, 38). She also likes new Coke. Experience and context are emphasized over other components. New TEE is anything that is contextualized leadership training. Nevertheless TEE requires some form of mediated instruction. Participant interaction is also expected for good learning as well as service and experience. The new Coke is not so different from the old.

In actuality there are other component parts in a TEE model. For example, the discussion group leader must be considered a component (see chapter one). In workshops conducted to train people unfamiliar with the TEE model, a large amount of instruction is given on the place of the discussion group leader (tutor/mentor).

A certain type of student is also an essential component of the process, for without adult participants rich in experience the model is incomplete. "Students come to TEE with experience in the areas being studied and so have an immediate context in which to place the material learned" (Esterline 1986, 3). Anjo Keikung, an Indian educator, confirms this when he states, "In TEE, the student is the focal point of teaching and learning. As such, all teaching techniques and learning materials are centered around the context of the student himself" (1985, 54).

Fred Holland adds spiritual foundation to the model (1983, 106). I interpret Holland as saying that the purpose of spiritual formation must be an understood component of TEE—a given. Weldon Viertel of the Caribbean Baptist Theological Education Association explains how a spiritual base is a must in TEE:

> Another source of motivation is the work of the indwelling Holy Spirit: "For it is God which worketh in you both to will and to do of his good pleasure" (Phil. 2:13). Persons who have a genuine call to minister and a commitment to the will of God can be expected to have greater motivation....the mysterious working of God's Spirit can bring about unexpected results. (1979, 36)

Jim and Carol Plueddemann also point to this spiritual dimension when they say, "Good methods for small groups use all the resources of the Holy Spirit—relating the experience of life with the authority of Scripture in interaction with other Christians" (1990, 55)

Holland illustrates the foundational aspect of the spiritual base. He likens the two parallel tracks of a railroad line to the self-study books and practical service of the student (1983, 106). The discussion seminars are represented by the sleepers or railroad ties. These ties lie in a bed of rock representing the spiritual foundation or base. The spiritual base is made up of the work of the Holy Spirit, desire of the students to study, their spiritual aspirations, and the goal of spiritual formation or development.

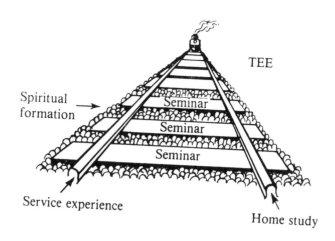

Figure 2. Railroad Track Analogy

Another foundational element of TEE is administration. My experience is that usually some space is devoted to this feature at the *end* of a workshop on TEE. By that time the participants have absorbed so much material that they cannot reflect adequately upon all that administration entails. Administration, when carefully studied and applied, greatly facilitates the program. In the early workshops administration was thought of as essential to TEE.

All these internal factors are the component parts of a truly contextual TEE. What cannot be fully appreciated in a mere listing is the praxis nature of the model. Independent study leads to individual reflection, the context of the student provides the setting for action, and peer group interaction in the seminar evolves into group reflection and finally praxis.

Original Design

TEE as a subset of Theological Education was originally proposed as an alternative to residence training. It began in Guatemala in the early sixties in response to a need for training clergy "on-the-job." The Presbyterian Church was getting so few pastors from among its seminary graduates that it decided to take the seminar to the students, with the expectation that contextual training in the students' culture would help them remain in their pastoral roles. The story is told by Ralph Winter, considered the father of the movement, in his book (1969).

The idea that natural leaders with spiritual gifts could be trained without removing them from their normal productive lives was revolutionary. The plan worked well, especially in rural areas where it was first applied. More pastors were trained, and they stayed with their churches.

The model of decentralized theological training goes back to the days when Methodist laypreachers learned to minister by doing. They read certain books, and periodically a circuit rider came by to discuss what they had learned and how they were putting it into practice (Holland 1978, 111–121).

TEE was originally designed with the model of a pastor-apprentice who learned by being coached on-the-job (Kinsler 1981, 9–12; Holland 1983). Pastors carried out serious theological studies distant from any academic institutions while conducting daily ministry. In the process these ministries grew in vitality. Since TEE was designed to train people who could not leave home to attend a Bible school or seminary, it was like a return to the pioneer days of the circuit rider.

The principle underlying the original model of TEE was that theological education could be made more relevant if done at the scene of action: the local church or place of ministry. The underlying educational philosophy was that students could put into immediate practice what they learned and avoid the gap associated with studying at a distant school and then going into ministry. TEE's philosophy was embodied in the slogan, "Training *in* ministry, and *for* ministry" (Holland 1980, 137–149).

Purposes of the Design

To find the original purposes of the design, it is necessary to examine the documents of the first eleven years of the movement. Several streams of thought converged in the model with much debate over function and learning materials (McKinney 1991).

The Presbyterian Seminary of Guatemala was not producing enough pastors for its rural churches. Many of the graduates remained in the cities in secular employment and did not return to pastoral ministry. The original purpose of some who undertook the creation of this new form of training was to abandon the pattern of residence school training and introduce TEE as a "decentralized training of ministers" (Winter 1969, 3–4).

Others, however, felt these two training models could be combined. Peter Savage wanted residential seminary training added to the extension program to advance the total ministry training (Covell and Wagner 1971, 78–79). C. Peter Wagner also felt that TEE and residence training could work together (Covell and Wagner 1971, 84–91). In his model all the extension classes were tied to a residence school, and professors from residence schools were the tutors for TEE. And in fact TEE took this actual form in some early programs. Some even said that "without residence schools it would be impossible to have extension programs" (Sprunger 1981, 133).

The Committee to Assist Missionary Education Overseas (CAMEO) sponsored workshops to initiate TEE programs. TEE was brought to the attention of missionaries and nationals in Africa and Asia for the first time at these workshops (Bates, 1971). Ward and Rowen, who conducted the first CAMEO workshops, laid a foundation in theory to support the superstructure of extension training (Covell and Wagner 1971, 119). They introduced programmed instruction and gave an overview of extension.

Holland says that while the original aim of TEE was the training of pastors who needed (and wanted) upgrading (1991), the further underlying aim was to train the ministry, which included the whole church, lay and pastoral. The leadership crisis in Africa was similar to that in Latin America—pastors were in short supply, as were trained local church workers. Pastoral training was in the forefront of the thinking of the founders to the point that anything less was downgraded as unworthy of TEE.

> I believe it is also important to underscore the fact that TEE is not just a glorified lay training program. In a typical lay training program, for example, little is expected of the student. TEE expects a lot . . . TEE aims mainly at the development of leaders and leadership gifts. (Sprunger 1981, 146)

James Emery says that its purpose was the "training of elders ... who carry the load of teaching, preaching, pastoral care and administration" (1969a, 13). Emery, however, stressed two other facets: to enhance and refine skills already manifest in mature laymen and to train people at the congregational level (16–17). They were "taught within the program of their own congregation" (Mulholland 1976, 99).

The occasion for the formation of TEE was the dearth of pastors prepared to shepherd churches, but the training of the whole body was also in mind from the beginning. Kinsler strongly asserts that the philosophy of TEE is the "understanding that the congregations themselves can and must form their own leaders and candidates for ordination" (1981, 92).

With the development of TEE came a much needed parallel emphasis on the plurality of leadership in the local churches. Milton G. Baker, one of main forces in the CAMEO workshops, sums up the original purpose:

> What is the basic purpose of a seminary extension program? It is *taking* training to people who have been given spiritual gifts, enabling them to better communicate the Gospel (1969, 263).

TEE challenged a one-person type of leadership and focused on numbers of local leaders, each with ministry gifts. Local church leadership was enhanced through extension.

Praxis Elements

The reflection-action-reflection pattern of TEE developed from its inception as professor and students interacted. Wagner summarizes the general pattern in the early days in this way:

> Several regional centers were thus set up, where the students would meet once a week with the professor from the seminary, receive help on his studies of the previous week, and take home assignments for the coming week. The same textbooks used (in the seminary) were the basis of the (new) study program. (Covell and Wagner 1971, 73)

Discussion developed even more because the student was in the midst of practical service and had many questions to bring to the session.

Students

From the start, all originators looked toward a particular kind of student. They wanted those who were highly motivated and serious about ministry. Most of the students were working for a living, and the theological education program could be adjusted to fit their schedule (Hopewell 1969, 44). Emery advocated that selection of students be made on the basis of experience as well as call (1969a, 18).

TEE met the need of those who could not leave home (Emery 1969a, 19). The advantage was that the student's roots in community were not lost. When students finished, they were still right at home and did not have to readjust. Also older, more established Christians would be given opportunity to study. Nevertheless, ordained pastors were not forgotten. Many of them would study in TEE as a form of continuing education (Mulholland 1976, 99).

The real genius of such a creative model was in its potential for contextualization. With discussion classes near home, students would more easily relate to their context. Winter expressed it cogently, "training for a local ordained pastoral role is relative to the situation in which that role must be performed" (1969, 34–35). Mulholland pointed out the contextual nature of the TEE model by saying, "review of assignment (is) followed by a discussion of questions raised by the student or teacher along with an application of the lesson *to the contemporary scene, his church and the world*" (1976, 143 italics mine).

Discussion Seminars

It took some time for the ideal of dialogical interaction between students to take shape. In the beginning, the seminar was a "research paper which he (the student) defended each week in private with his tutor" (Hopewell 1969, 47). The educative model of the seminary did not change in the first TEE classes. Yet discussion was not long in coming. The seminars soon became places where self-expression was an important part of learning. The fellowship at center meetings became more central to the model (Winter 1969, 96)

The tutor (called originally the "professor") was to maintain personal contact with students in the weekly seminar meeting. Sometimes this took the form of counseling and trouble shooting as much as discussion (Winter 1969, 92). The tutor, now more frequently called the center leader, was not to duplicate a traditional classroom model. Savage graphically describes the tutor as "a midwife, helping the student to bring to birth biblical truth in his heart and mind" (Mulholland 1976, 67). The professors' role in TEE was to help the student struggle with biblical concepts and apply them.

Self-study texts

Originally there were no self-study texts. Assignments were given much as in a traditional school. This meant that a great reliance was placed on reading and self-study (Winter 1969, 44). Before any programmed texts became available, texts were glorified workbooks "keyed to the Bible or basic theological books because take-home studies were hard to digest with students of limited reading ability" (Mulholland 1976, 80). Hopewell wanted to see good books in every language of study (1969, 47).

One important hope of early practitioners was that programmed texts "would help students learn how to think" (Mulholland 1976, 116). A. M. Gustafson put programmed materials in the center of the TEE model when he said,

> What we have in mind is an Extension Seminary where the teacher goes to the pupil and teaches him in his setting. This requires planned and prepared material programmed in such a way that the pupil can study by himself, and have the teacher visit him once a week for instruction and tests in the lesson studied. (1969, 201)

Esterline sums up the early attitude of the initiators of TEE, "Educational technology was looked to by many early TEE enthusiasts in the attempt to create a thoroughly competent match for residential education" (1986, 91).

Programmed instruction had much to offer for content input, but was an enormous project. This task was undertaken by industrious missionaries working together with nationals on all five continents. McKinney led one of the most extensive writing projects in Latin America (1975); Fred and Grace Holland's TEXT Africa project is the largest on that continent. The need for more national writers to insure adequate contextualization became evident (Mulholland 1976, 90). After a time enthusiasm for programming was lost because Christian educators found fault with Skinner's behavioristic model.

Wagner overstated the "book is your teacher" philosophy when he said, "The 'professors' in extension education are really the semi-programmed textbooks which are being written in Spanish to cover the entire theological curriculum" (1969, 280). Whether a book can "teach" or not is debatable. Distance educators, as we have seen, view the written material as encoded conversation between teacher and pupil.

Structures of Early Programs

The extension concept from the beginning was decentralized education, a school without walls. Contact with the students was weekly (Winter 1969, 25), which was seen at first as a distinct disadvantage (Emery 1969b, 99) since residence afforded daily contact. Wagner pointed out, however, that frequently professors at seminaries were too busy to give much time to students (Covell and Wagner 1971, 93), while TEE was personal and concentrated. Meetings were to be in centers, which might be a church or home. Some of the things which were envisioned have persisted; others have fallen away.

Features which have persisted include: the periodic discussion class, students purchase their own textbooks, modification in the styles of independent study materials, different academic levels studying together, block scheduling of seminars, flexible time periods for the completion of studies, and yearly convocations.

Some of the things which have fallen away or are infrequently seen are monthly gatherings at a central location for all students, academically qualified seminar leaders, and required sermon outlines handed in weekly.

Emery describes the first TEE effort in Guatemala. It began with a two-week institute in which the subject matter was introduced to students. It included monthly visits to the seminary by the students, and visits of faculty members to the students. Personnel without degrees were not qualified to lead TEE classes. A library of resources also played a part in the original design. Visits to the seminary afforded students time for research. At the end of the year there was a general review at the seminary, and exams were given (Emery 1969a, 19). Mulholland adapts a diagram from Winter's book to explain the flow of the original model (1976, 71).

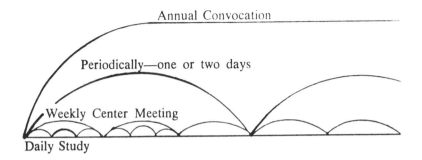

Figure 3. Flow of Original Model

Problems and Issues

Many problems and issues involved the relationship of TEE administration to the churches with which it works. Often, the missing ingredient is consultation with the church (or stakeholders) involved. When TEE administrators do not get the input of the church in such matters as curriculum, accreditation, evaluation, and finances, serious problems with the program often result.

Curriculum

Curriculum problems were germinal in the inception of extension. At first, traditional theological curriculum was used. Soon, however, people not in full-time ministry, including people of lower educational levels, began enrolling and needed upgrading to do the theological studies. This led to curriculum adjustments. Sometimes the church sponsored secular education to raise the educational level of the student (Winter 1969, 45–69).

Accreditation

Accreditation was in the minds of the originators of TEE from the very beginning. Holland wrote to Ray Buker on the eve of the first Association of Evangelical Bible Institutes and Colleges of Africa and Madagascar (forerunner of AEAM) workshops and listed this among concerns (1970). Winter very creatively set accreditation forth on the basis of function, not academia (1969, 30f). While functional equivalence is just beginning to surface now, as early as 1966 Winter was talking of the "functional equivalence" of various levels of training. His exact words are worth quoting:

> It is the question of whether ordination must be based on some absolute standard of knowledge and be the same for everyone, everywhere, or whether ordination should be based on an education that is only functionally equivalent across time and space. Can different academic levels be functionally equivalent? (1969, 30)

Evaluation

While little has been written on the evaluation of TEE, several important books and articles are available. Patricia Harrison said, "TEE is not always easy to evaluate, since it varies enormously in goals, methods, and ethos" (1990, 28). TEE is a very flexible model, suited to fit into diverse situations. A special strength like this, however, demands careful handling and regular evaluation. But evaluation has been emphasized only since the third period in the historical development of TEE, 1984 to the present. The originators were busy developing the model, not setting standards for its evaluation. Nevertheless, early in the development of TEE some saw the importance of evaluation. Harrison implies that this must include even the setting up of the program:

> There have been some skyrocket programs—a sudden 'big bang' launching, a riot of exciting noises, lights and colors, and a rapid fizzle into oblivion. Often such programs fail because the necessary pre-launch work has not been done. (1977, 6)

Since the 1984 consultation on TEE at Cyprus, TEE has been undergoing evaluation both spoken and written. The danger of anecdotal evidence is that it may be based on inadequate research. Definite criteria are needful to prevent evaluation of TEE programs on the basis of anecdotal evidence. But formative evaluation is clearly needed, because programs have broken down.

Leaders at the ACTEA All Africa Conference of Theological Educators (Kenya, May 30-June 3, 1990) held three symposiums based on Mulholland's assessment of TEE (1984, 17–18) containing a list of weaknesses that David Kornfield set forth. The result was a four-page paper in which twenty-three recommendations were proposed to the ACTEA commission to help African TEE programs (ACTEA 1990, 4). See Appendix B.

Criteria of Evaluation
Summarized below are five principal accomplishments of TEE listed by Mulholland (1984, 13–16) each of which indicate a criterion for evaluation:

1. *Availability.* TEE has made formal theological training available to persons to whom it was previously unavailable.

2. *Educational Methodology.* TEE has raised significant issues of educational methodology.

3. *Creativity.* TEE has unleashed unparalleled creativity in theological education at all levels.

4. *Strengthened the Church.* TEE has strengthened the church numerically and in spiritual growth.

5. *Leadership Selection.* TEE has brought to the forefront the question of leadership selection.

Developing Servant Leadership
The kind of leaders a training program produces often reveals the efficacy of that program. Servant leaders are in demand. The development of Christ-like individuals correlates with Mulholland's fifth point, leadership selection. If the right kind of participants are selected, a better chance exists for the right product to result.

The criteria for evaluating theological education is whether or not it develops servant leaders who are filled with the Spirit of Christ, faithful to the Word and the church (Ferris 1978, 9).

Developing Gifted People
Many people whose potential is not tapped have spiritual gifts in the church. A criterion of evaluation is the development and display of such gifts. This parallels the development of skills in personnel in a secular job. Once we see gifted people emerging from the shadows of church oblivion, we can acclaim a program's effectiveness.

Ward says that development of gifts, not numbers, should be the major criterion of TEE's effectiveness. "The larger issue is what is being done for the people of God. If TEE facilitates a wide recognition and development of the gifts of the Spirit, it seems appropriate for continued support and encouragement" (1974, 257).

Developing Church Ownership

An evaluation of how the chosen TEE program has affected the church would also serve as a good starting place for standards or criteria. This echoes loudly with the fourth accomplishment listed above: TEE has strengthened the church. Since the church is the primary community served by TEE, it must have a voice in setting criteria for evaluation. Ralph R. Covell notes that there is no better context in which to evaluate mature students than in the church context. "Therefore evaluation can be done by members of the church they are serving. This evaluation is much more complete, because the church is able to see the student in the total environment in which he is living" (Covell and Wagner 1971, 40).

Risks of Initiating TEE

A risk exists in running TEE programs solely from missionary perspective with little church control. The church needs to be involved from the inception of the program. "Too often programs have been started on the initiative of a single missionary, with little goal ownership on the part of the national church" (Mulholland 1984, 21). National church involvement and ownership is a key criterion in evaluating TEE.

Ferris says that the essence of TEE is not in methodology but in the distinctive context (the church) in which ministry formation is undertaken (1984, 52). Thus TEE needs to maintain its original church-based design and evaluation must proceed accordingly.

> It is imperative that we develop ministry training structures with (rather than for) the church, therefore, because it is only through participation of the church that those structures are endowed with meaning and value. (Ferris 1984, 55)

Church Control

Thus, any evaluation which does not begin with church-based criteria misses the whole point. As Ferris says, "For ministry training to serve the church, it (TEE) must belong to the church. It must be controlled by the church" (1984, 54). To reach this stage, however, dialogical interaction between missionaries and national leaders must develop, and a true flow of thought from one to the other must take place. Only through true interaction can models be adjusted to fit the host culture and be owned by church leaders.

The degree of church control of a ministry is proportionate to the involvement and commitment of its people. If the training logistics are too difficult to be carried out, the national church cannot be blamed if it does not adopt the training-model wholeheartedly (Mulholland 1984, 21). The church needs to be a wholehearted participant in the endeavor.

Efforts to *sell* the program need careful consideration of insider opinion makers. Leaders of the church must understand what is involved in a TEE program, its costs, and the commitment necessary for students to participate. They also need to share in the creation of expected outcomes.

The church can neither sit back and let leadership training happen nor can it just demand authority to control. A true meeting of minds must take place to help the church devise a training strategy that is truly contextual, one that is not only acceptable but productive. The church must be able to make sense out of the model of training and run it on their own (cf. Ward 1974, 258). "...Only as they (leaders-in-training) see the church assuming ownership and control of training can they be assured that their ministry will be accepted by the church (Ferris 1984, 55).

Developing Goals of a Program

Having enunciated the importance of church related evaluation, one must consider the goals the church has for the program. The church must direct the goals of the program, so that these two juxtapose. Harrison explains that we can only answer the question, "Does TEE work?" by examining goals.

> It is meaningful only to talk about particular TEE programs and to evaluate these in terms of their own goals. The goals in turn would be subject to evaluation in terms of actual needs in the church and community being served. (Harrison 1977, 4)

Bradley Hill shows how deeper church involvement with TEE programs is the path to greater ownership by the church, making a meaningful training model (1988, 46–47). He shows that if the church helps to write courses and plan the program, this will be the key to the development of a feeling of ownership.

Kiranga Gatimu, coordinator of the Eastern Africa Association for Theological Education by Extension (EAATEE) is concerned about evaluation and the attitude of church leaders,

> (who) are not fully committed to TEE as most of them do not understand it. Indeed, if it were not for the availability of expatriate personnel and their funds, it is likely that few TEE programmes would have started in Africa purely on the initiative of national leaders alone. (1985, 3)

Church leaders need to grapple with goals of the TEE program as stakeholders or sponsors. By contributing criteria of what they as leaders desire, the goals of a specific program can be evaluated more precisely. Their input makes program goals relative to the church.

Setting and Measuring Criteria

TEE needs not only the setting of criteria, but instruments to measure program goals. Harvie Conn says that "no in-depth evaluative criteria have yet been developed to determine to what extent extension education is filling the needs of the church" (1984, 270). But this will soon change.

Esterline wrote his dissertation (1986) as "A Proposal for the Evaluation of Theological Education by Extension". He includes a 41-page evaluation workbook in his dissertation (171–212) well worth using because of its thoroughness. He stresses criteria developed from community (church) input and from how the needs of the church are being met. "Values determined by the Bible, by the needs of the community or by the special interests of a specific group . . . form the center of the evaluation . . ." (1986, 147). This type of evaluation does not depend on opinion outside the church.

Evaluation must also consider the flexibility of the TEE model. It must be formative so that TEE can make midcourse corrections. "The program must never stagnate or crystalize—it must remain pliable, constantly adapting to new situations and correcting past shortcomings" (Covell and Wagner 1971, 75).

Finances

Finances have always been an issue. Historically, finances were used as a major point in favor of TEE. When students stopped coming to the seminary, two large financial items relating to residence schools—that is, maintenance of the plant and food for the students—were completely avoided.

Outside funding helped TEE get its start in many countries. The Theological Education Fund provided capital for the beginning of the TEE work in Latin America. The major costs became preparation of materials and transport of teachers. These remain as problems today, and surface along with other financial concerns in the case studies of chapters six through ten.

Sometimes finances became an issue between the church and program. Mulholland gives an example of a church summarily taking funds from a TEE budget (1976, 155). TEE administrators frequently complain about lack of church funding of the program, as we will see in chapter four. An underlying reason for this is suggested in the above discussion on evaluation—that the church needs to be in on the ground floor of program development, including finances. One of the early problems was convincing the church of the value of the extension program so that they *would* finance it. Winter's whole book (1969) was an apologetic for the TEE movement to the Presbyterian Church. Relationship with the mother church is still crucial to financing TEE programs today.

Residence and/or Extension

The early polarization of extension versus residence schools discussed earlier in this chapter still has overtones today. Though the existence of residence and extension as divisions of the same institution was considered ideal, there still remains much uncertainty today. Extension seminaries should be viewed not as threats to present structures, but as meeting a need that the residence schools were not fulfilling (Covell and Wagner 1971, 8).

Self-study material

In the early days, there was experimentation with different types of material, including a comic strip format by George Patterson in Honduras (Mulholland 1976, 151–152). Many felt that programmed instruction would facilitate the TEE praxis, and massive production efforts were carried on through programs initiated by AETTE in Brazil, AEAM in Africa, PAFTEE in the Philippines, and TAFTEE in India.

But questions emerged as to the effectiveness and design of programmed texts, although thousands of students have learned through them demonstrating that the programmed books can teach content. Ted and Margaret Ward held high hopes for programmed books.

> What is important is that some materials will become available and will be used, evaluated, and revised and then will become both encouragement, stimulation, and models for even more and finer materials. This could be the start of something very important in the field of extension education and theological education across the world. (1970, 3)

While programmed books can teach content, they cannot do everything a human teacher would do. From this the issue arose regarding the phrase "the book is your teacher" used of programmed books. Interestingly, in the Guatemalan model, the phrase was not, "the book is your teacher," but rather, "each book is a teacher" (Walker 1969, 552). The originators did not see the human teacher being replaced by a book. Holland emphasized the importance of the seminar leader (1975, 21–22) not as a giver of information (which is the book's function) but as a resource person interacting with the student. Much misunderstanding could have been avoided in later years had this original understanding been preserved.

In the period of origination, a warning was sounded that programmed instruction should not be the sole source of cognitive instruction. "... programming strategies should lead toward independence rather than dependence. The programmed instruction should not become the perpetual crutch without which the student cannot or will not learn for himself" (Ward and Ward 1970, 4). Programmed books should teach the students pastoral and ministry skills so they can develop that independence. No law prevents TEE students from being exposed to and using other methods of study as self-directed learners.

Evangelism

Another underlying principle was that TEE would be used with an active program of evangelism in the local church. Patterson in his book *Obedience Oriented Education* (1976) premised his whole program on the condition that students do evangelism and plant churches.

Although often not spelled out as finely or as well as Patterson's plan, all TEE was geared to the simple but vital concern that students do evangelism.

Theological educators were hoping that TEE would cure all training ills. But TEE has to be rightly related to certain processes to have effect. One of these processes is evangelism. Patterson's concern was that his classes be related to the community via active evangelism, so that the ideal might be fulfilled. Therefore he limited each of his classes to six students only and required that each student do evangelism and plant a church (1976).

"TEE is not designed to *stand alone* as a panacea for all church problems. It is designed primarily to come alongside and help Christians already motivated to Bible study and Christian service" (Snook 1980, 2). TEE was never begun as just an academic program.

> Joined with an ongoing program of evangelism in a local church TEE insures success. But TEE without a concurrent evangelism program may just become another way to do formal schooling. Remember TEE needs an active evangelistic program in a local church to fulfill its potential. It cannot do it alone. (Snook 1980, 3)

Theoretical Philosophy of TEE

Place of Training

The locus of training was heavily emphasized in the theory behind TEE. Students were trained among the people. They were serving in real life situations. Kinsler stressed the need to train people in the environment of their church and society (1981, 15–17). The theory was that since the application could be made immediately, real learning was more likely to take place. Knowledge was not stored somewhere in a filing cabinet in hopes that it would be used someday.

Active in Ministry

The TEE philosophy of training was that students were to be active in ministry, not removed from that ministry, and therefore church leaders would not have the problem of placing the graduates. Graduates would not drop out of service, they would remain on the scene in the church (even if they did not complete the training). The reason behind this philosophy was that students would have a greater interest in their studies because of the possibility of immediate application to their ministries. They would perceive it as useful to their purposes. Thus, the one studying would integrate his theological learning into church life without delay.

Patterson lists five conditions for a theological education program to keep people active in ministry (1976, 20):

1. Directly related to the local church.
2. Fits the needs of the local church.
3. Permits spontaneous expansion of the church.
4. Trains others in a chain according to 2 Tim. 2:2.
5. Builds into its program a workable system of accountability.

An active ministry in the church context is central to the philosophy of TEE.

Real Problems

Because of the locus of training (their communities, churches and homes), students grapple with problems in real life. Tutors do not need to resort to simulations and hypothetical problems. The concern of education is to equip leaders to face the world, solve problems, and meet the church's needs from the eternal perspective of the Word of God. Only through the Word of God can we develop sound judgment to face life.

In TEE, the discussion class is designed to help participants grapple dialogically with real problems in a very imperfect world. Through interaction, God's people learn to think and express themselves. They learn how to solve problems and overcome obstacles. The theory of TEE is grounded in these sound educational principles (cf. Covell and Wagner 1971, 101-109).

Cultural Dislocation and Placement

Another intended value of TEE philosophy is avoidance of cultural dislocation. When students left their homes to attend a residence or day school, they learned a new way of life and often found it difficult to fit in once again among their own people.

The first TEE writers stressed that to urbanize a student from a rural area frequently makes that student incapable of readjusting to rural or village life again (Winter 1969; Covell and Wagner 1971; Kinsler 1981). If students were uprooted from their jobs, and the church could not pay them a living wage, it would be hard for them to reacclimate to the situation. No doubt three years of Bible school or College do change individuals, but if the education process dislocates them culturally, they may find it difficult to readjust to their home situation for ministry.

The philosophy of TEE asserts that the difficulties of post-graduate placement can be alleviated by training individuals where they are already accepted as natural or potential leaders. Many national and mission leaders can testify to the difficulty of getting young Bible school graduates placed in churches where they are not known. I personally can testify to several cases of Bible school graduates who did not last more than two or three years because of acceptance problems. One church in Soweto, South Africa went through three young pastors from Bible school, then decided to use their own local people. If the accepted leaders from such a local church had been trained in their own context rather than relocating them, the church may have circumvented this problem because those leaders already had acceptance by their own people.

Functional Leadership in the Local Church

The theory of TEE training is important for the sake of functional leadership in the local church. The tendency is to train national leadership beyond the capacity of the local church to support it. The ideal of TEE is that leaders who are doing ministry in the church can study while they remain in their gainful employment.

Church leaders who want training are not extracted from their normal productive lives, yet they are enabled to develop their spiritual gifts in ministry. Thus TEE was designed to be contextual right from the start. Both the self-study material and the discussion classes were tailored to help leaders within their local ministry.

When TEE came on the scene there were great expectations that it would work where residence education was falling short. TEE moved ahead with limited materials eager to try out the new approach. Since TEE is designed to train a functional leadership, questions like: "Is it getting the job done?" and "Are functional leaders being trained in local churches?" were critical to its development.

TEE's original approach of functionality is vitally important beause residential schools are also seeing the importance of practical experience in ministry as central to learning.

In the next chapter, I move from a review of TEE literature to the views of thirty TEE administrators in Africa on how their programs are developing today.

CHAPTER FOUR

Signals of Success

Different people have different views or standards of what success or effectiveness is. In a weight reduction program, people want to lose different amounts of weight. Some may lose slowly. Others may be able to lose weight in a shorter period of time. For some, five pounds loss is a success; for others, ten pounds instead of twenty is failure.

Effectiveness or success can only be measured by the goals set. Evaluation takes place when achievement is measured against those goals.

The focus here is what thirty representative TEE administrators throughout Africa reported in a preliminary open-ended questionnaire as effective or not effective in their programs, achievement measured against their goals. (Note that q=questionnaire in Appendix C. All abbreviations are listed on pages v and vi.)

Hitting the Mark

Six broad areas emerged as hitting the mark of success. These comprise:

1. expanding programs
2. church growth
3. developing leaders
4. growth of individuals
5. acceptance by the church
6. evangelism

Expanding Programs

Questionnaire respondents wrote: "many students are continuing to take courses," "enrollment is increasing," "more students are gaining certificates," and "additional classes have been requested." Programs are apparently successful if there is an ongoing and increasing demand for them. Success breeds success. A school with interested students attracts more students. The increasing demand for classes and the number of students indicate that there is a desire on the part of many church people in Africa to study the Word of God through TEE.

Growing Churches

Church growth was given as an evidence of success for several programs. TEE was not always stated as the sole cause for the growth, but was a correlated factor.

Here are some expressions of TEE and church growth: "more people are attending local churches because TEE students encourage everyone to be interested," and (more than once) "the growth of churches is in direct relationship to the work of the TEE students." Active participation of TEE students in the churches and evangelization by students were common elements affective to the growth pattern.

Others indicated that TEE students had begun new churches, among them Margaret Thornton of the Anglican diocese of Nakuru, Kenya: "Four new congregations have been started by lay people in the last three years. We have an average of 60 TEE groups a term, each based in a church, and it would be true to say all those churches have grown in one way or another" (CPKLTP 1990q). ICM in Kenya says, "We have seen six new churches planted due to the influence of TEE" (1990q).

Roger Erickson writes that multiple new churches have been planted due to the work of TEE students in Ethiopia. In an article in *Global Church Growth,* he attributes church growth directly to the active TEE students (1989, 1).

Developing Leaders

TEE helps those who are already seeking to work for the Lord in their churches and provides an opportunity for training which would not otherwise be available. In many cases TEE is the only Christian education program the church has. Students trained in TEE multiply themselves by teaching others what they have learned.

Aseffa Jatey, national supervisor of the Baptist TEE program in Ethiopia, says that TEE is successful in his church "because the program is training lay leaders of the churches who are not only involved in evangelism, church planting and discipling, but who are (also) training others in the same (way)" (BEATEE 1990q). Many leaders see evidence that TEE is fulfilling the needs of Bible study and leadership training in their churches.

Growth of Individual

Another mark of success has been individual growth in faith, character, and the ability to transfer truth to others. Testimonies abound of students who show personal growth and development in their lives as a result of studying through TEE. Administrators mention enthusiasm, changed lives, greater faithfulness, and active participation in the church as qualities of their students.

Some have grown professionally, becoming pastors. Naboth Mtangodura says, "Many of our local churches have no trained pastors. They are being shepherded by our TEE students, some of whom have now graduated from the assigned set of courses" (EBC-TEE 1990q). Others also indicate that many trained lay leaders are getting the burden to enter the pastorate and are becoming full-time pastors.

Acceptance by the Church

Does it seem strange to you that TEE administrators would list acceptance by the church as a mark of success? Conversely, non-acceptance by the church (as a denomination) heads the list as cause for lack of success. When the denomination accepts TEE as an official training program in its churches, it gives a mighty push towards success. The battle for acceptance has been so difficult that when a church does accept TEE, administrators consider that their program will succeed. "Interest in TEE is at an all-time high. The program now has the complete support of the church" says David Harvey (MPE 1990q) of the Mission Protestante-Evangelique TEE of Cote d'Ivoire.

Acceptance of TEE by the church as a "form of leadership training" is a mark of success. In these instances, TEE has satisfied the stakeholders, namely the church leaders, of the viability of the program. Julie Fehr claims that "99% of local C&MA churches" have involvement in TEE in Gabon (ETD 1990q).

Evangelism

Evangelism gives TEE a solid measure of its effectiveness. It is the most talked-about item by administrators, appearing again and again as the focus of student activity. This response is borne out by other research. In a questionnaire used in urban and rural Kenya, 90% of the students reported that TEE has helped them lead someone to the Lord (Urbanization 1990, 6). TEE students are motivated to do evangelism, and they testify spontaneously to the opportunities they have to witness and win others to the Lord. Pochi says, "We have succeeded in training over 10,000 people. The people are now more evangelistic than ever" (COCIN-EBS 1990q). In every instance where the administrators mention church planting, evangelism is there—the assured component of church planting.

Contextualization and TEE

A working definition of contextualization stresses the ability of missionaries and national leaders to make the teachings of God's Word relevant to the culture in which they are immersed. The degree to which this has been accomplished in any single instance is often baffling for educators to determine. Applying the Bible to all aspects of life is a demanding and arduous process. Although administrators report on contextualization as an important accomplishment of TEE, it is one which leaders must always keep in the forefront—honing and integrating this skill.

An Indian educator points out that TEE stands for innovation in theological education, enabling church members to study at home in the context of the local church while developing approaches to teaching and learning. Indeed (extension) is a contextual theological education. (Keikung 1986, 83)

While some TEE administrators answering the open-ended questionnaire either did not know or felt their program was too new to judge the extent of contextualization, 70% polled felt their program was conducive to contextualization. These leaders indicated that five overt activities were particularly expressive of contextualization: use of tests which help the process, testimonies of students, confronting witchcraft and ancestor worship, witness within the community, and items discussed in seminars.

Use of Texts

The AEAM programmed texts include many attempts at contextualizing the truth of Scripture. Some texts have as many as fifty references to African culture which serve as levers for the African Christians to help others understand the Gospel in their culture.

Jim Lo quotes a church leader who exclaims, "TEE makes it easy for me to understand the Bible." Lo goes on to share, "The numerous stories and illustrations in the African context have been beneficial in getting the people to see Christianity as African and directly related to their spiritual work" (EWBSE 1990q).

A national leader from Ethiopia says that AEAM has "attempted to adapt texts to Ethiopian culture. People are coming to know and follow Christ through the ministries of TEE program participants and graduates...One reason for this is the ability of people to understand the Gospel *in their contexts*" (BEATEE 1990q).

Discussion questions in the AEAM Text-Africa series were written by those with experience in Africa. Administrators recognize this: "The courses prepared by AEAM give attention to contextualization in the discussion questions" (CEAZ-ETD 1990q).

Testimonies of Participants

Respondents mentioned testimonies as an empirical evidence that African Christians are using what they learn in a way their fellow citizens understand; participants often evince contextualization in their testimonies.

"I hear them witnessing and telling the good of it (TEE) during conventions. Especially during the certificate-giving day, once or twice a year for every center" (KAGE 1990q). Others mention that testimonies at the baptism of new converts reveal contextualized understanding of the Gospel. Many testify that they have been able to lead their relatives to the Lord because of new insights from the discussion classes in TEE or an illustration from a self-study text.

Some of the strongest evidence of contextualization is given in testimonies of change in family life. Motsapi had been molded by the set-up in South Africa where men often work, as he did, 250 miles from home, returning infrequently to visit family.

While studying the Christian Home in TEE, a change first took place in his own life. As he taught these principles to his family and church on visits home, a change occurred in his wife as well, and many of their personal family problems were resolved by Scriptural application. He then decided to return home and live with his family instead of making more money in the city, feeling that money or no money, God's will for the family is that married people live together. His influence is now spreading to others in the community. Contextualization does not mean conformity to a culture, but modeling of Scriptural truth within that culture.

Witchcraft and Ancestor Worship

A leader from Zaire writes concerning his TEE class, "I know students have taken a stand against the fears and practice of witchcraft that some Christians still give in to under pressure" (CECA-ETE 1990q). Such a testimony is encouraging because good contextualization confronts syncretism.

Studying the AEAM text on prayer, students in our class discussed the fact that for many Africans, when medical doctors fail to heal, it is time to turn to the witchdoctor. But as Christians, we seek God and His will for us.

One woman testified later, "The (medical) doctor told me that my illness cannot be cured. I must take this medicine the rest of my life. My neighbor said, 'Come to the witchdoctor with me.' But I said, 'No. If God wants to heal me, He will heal me. But if not, then He will give me the grace to live like this and witness for Him.'"

Another man in our class gave a testimony that his neighbor lady was ill and not responding to (medical) treatment. Her family decided to call in the witchdoctor. But she said, "No, call my neighbor. He knows how to pray to God." Our student visited her that evening, and led her to the Lord.

Anita Johnson, former leader of the Phumelela Extension Bible School says that participants "understand ancestor worship better from studying the (TEE) books. In discussion...(they confront) the dangers of ancestor worship" (PBSE 1990q).

Many African Christians come to terms with issues related to ancestors. They have distinguished between honoring their parents and worship which is due only to God. Because TEE texts and discussion deal with grass roots issues in a respectful and contextualized manner, African Christians are helped.

Witness to the Community

Since TEE reaches church leaders in their own communities, contextualization takes place more easily. "Students are living the Gospel as they mix with others in their community. That is where others are attracted to the all sufficiency of the Gospel" (SAN 1990q).

Pochi of COCIN says that through TEE many more people in the villages are being reached. Students give reports of how they go about witnessing to the people. From Cote d'Ivoire comes the statement that contextualization is taking place *in creating a more extensive Gospel awareness* (MPE 1990q, italics mine). When TEE participants relate well to their own people and share the Gospel effectively with them, contextualization is at work.

Another important facet is enunciated: "Many of the PI (AEAM programmed instruction) texts emphasize field work—more than just theory. Students share their faith because they are always working with people, many of them sinners" (COCIN-EBS 1990q). When TEE participants go out "witnessing and speaking the good news in their own terms and language" contextualization takes place (MTS 1990q).

Discussion Seminars

The weekly discussion seminars buzz with practical contextualizing which comes right out of the experience of the student (CEAZ-ETD 1990q). Oral feedback is abundant in the discussion groups. Participants share what has happened to them and in the process reveal how they are contextualizing God's Word. The group also checks tendencies toward syncretism. One leader comments, "Having sat in on discussion classes...it is obvious that they are using what they are learning on a day by day basis" (BEATEE 1990q).

The utilization of truth in the participant's own context indicates a process delicately guided by the Holy Spirit. In this experience, the eyes of the understanding are truly opened, both for the participants and those who receive their witness.

Another leader stresses the fact that "the TEE set up...allows for students to discuss freely among themselves...an excellent forum for talking biblically about church, societal and family problems in a contextualized manner" (IBE 1990q). The mortar of contextualization is the discussion group; the pestle is the Word of God.

Causes of Breakdown

Not all TEE administrators feel their program is an "unqualified success." Some downgrade it to "marginally successful." Others list problems that have hindered progress. Since TEE programs do succeed in many instances, we need to examine the reported problems and causes of breakdown.

Listed here are possible causes for breakdown of TEE programs in Africa. The thirty programs in this survey are representative of programs throughout sub-Saharan Africa. While these problems do cause breakdown of the program, they are just that—problems—and as such, can and often have been overcome. In many cases, even though problems were present and hindering the work, yet there was a sense of limited success in the face of it all. In only two instances were programs listed as failing; and only one was on the verge of breakdown (and that because of a church-mission schism). Therefore let us look carefully at the following problems and view them as obstacles to overcome: lack of finances, lack of program structure, lack of trained leaders, preconceived ideas about TEE, and lack of church acceptance and approval.

Lack of Finances

Finances were reported as the number one problem. This includes such items as cost of books, salary for administrators, and incentives for class leaders. Education of all types requires funding—colleges and seminaries do—and so does TEE. One administrator said, "TEE may be cheaper than residence schools, but it is not cheap."

Although a primary cost item is production and translation of materials, this was not mentioned. The focus was on the student—what does it cost the student? That is the problem. The student must pay for his books. Said one, "Our program is not a total success, since we don't have enough money for manuals." *Not enough money*—that is the cry, despite book subsidy.

In Zaire where inflation is rampant, programs are in danger of collapsing from delay in getting books and the exorbitant cost of getting them through customs. *Creative solutions* are needed to develop less costly books, lower prices of existing books, and possibly to produce them locally to circumvent transportation and customs costs.

The second financial concern is funding for administrators and intermediary supervisors. I saw the results firsthand as one large TEE program lost funding for its intermediary supervisors. The program was definitely hampered as supervisors were unable to get to class sites, and discussion group leaders were left to function as best they could on their own. Grants and outside funding are two sources that could make a difference, and church subsidy is another.

Another trouble spot is transportation. TEE is a decentralized form of training. The leader goes where the students are, sometimes far distant and out of reach of public means of transport. Transport is costly, hence financial needs arise. Funds need to be raised for vehicles, bikes, or motorbikes for the TEE leaders who travel.

Lack of Program Structure

When a TEE principal complains of "lack of clear... structure," and "administration (which) does not facilitate the process," he is focusing on a formidable barrier to the progress of TEE. For example, the program may not provide for processing of student results in a central location. Books may be difficult to obtain or the ones which are translated too few to complete a module.

A leader in Zaire told me they had to wait a long time before they got the next book. Lack of "quick communication" (as one principal put it) hinders the schedule of ongoing classes. Zealous students are thwarted when communications break down, books are not delivered, and other administrative tasks are not performed when needed.

Dropouts are not a good advertisement for any program. When the TEE structure is not tight enough to decrease the attrition rate, we create a "big back door." The administrative structure should work to slow the attrition rate, not increase it.

Lack of Trained Leaders

The outcry from administrators who lack sufficiently well-trained dedicated leaders for their TEE programs is startling: "There are not enough people in leadership. We never had a full-time leader."

A program as complex as TEE cannot carry on without a full-time leader. When there is no leader, for whatever reason (sometimes a wonderful leader has to move away, with no one available to replace him), and there is no *good* solution, *bad* solutions follow.

One such "bad" solution is the overwork of those involved. One principal cries out, "I am having to do the work of five people myself." A toll is taken on the servant of God in such situations. Another TEE leader translates the books, holds training seminars for leaders, teaches classes, corrects the tests, and is responsible for all the administration. No wonder he suffers from high blood pressure.

Another bad solution is to appoint leaders who lack training and dedication and who do a poor job. Administrators talk of classes prospering when there is a strong, dedicated, enthusiastic discussion group leader; whereas if the leader is weak, uninformed and unfaithful (and in some cases does not even show up), the class will decline. This is not surprising, but it does point up the central role played by the discussion group leader. The saddest case I discovered was an administrator who admitted: "The program has struggled under six directors in ten years; (there are) *no informed leaders."*

The only thing worse than having no leader, or a constant change of leaders, is to have a leader who is not in sympathy with the program. One TEE program began to slide downhill because they appointed as leader a person who was not really convinced of TEE educational philosophy. You can imagine what happened to that program!

A complex educational model like TEE needs competent group-discussion facilitators. This problem, central to the stability of any TEE program, demands that we give thought to solving it.

A solution used by ETD in Gabon is a system of apprenticeship (assistant tutoring) for any who have studied eight TEE courses and take the basic leader's course. Following such a practice may be helpful for other programs struggling with problems of maintaining an adequately trained leadership. More will be said about both discussion groups and their leaders in the case studies of chapters six through ten.

Preconceived Ideas about TEE

Many people have only the vaguest idea of what TEE is, yet pronounce unfounded judgments upon it. These need to be counteracted with knowledge.

That TEE is an inferior form of Bible education is one such ill-informed judgment. TEE books are programmed for small-step learning. Someone untrained in such a technique may not realize that small steps take the learner far into knowledge of Scripture. A test of basic Bible knowledge given to both Bible School students and TEE students, shows the truth—TEE students do not fall behind in Bible knowledge.

Also, basic vocabulary is used in the first level TEE studies to facilitate translation and accommodate students unaccustomed to difficult reading. One accustomed to suppose that big truths can only be taught with lengthy words will be tempted to misjudge the material used in TEE. If people need to be trained where they are, instead of going away to another locality, suitable instructional material needs to be produced for them. The discussion group leader can introduce additional higher level material as suitable to the class.

One administrator wrote, "The idea among most pastors (is) that three years at a residential Bible school is the only way a pastor can be trained." This misconception hinders the start of new programs.

Residential and extension schools have learned to get along together, but it is taking the church a while to catch up with the reconciliation. In 1989 a church with an active extension program ordained its first "lay evangelist" after he took 27 TEE courses and led a local church for five years. He is proving to be an effective pastor. Another church has ordained into the ministry its first solely TEE-trained student. As churches continue to do this, people will understand more fully their options for training under TEE.

Lack of Church Acceptance and Approval

The greatest obstacle to TEE which I found in my research is lack of formal acceptance and approval by denominations and missions. When leadership officially adopts TEE as a program and actively promotes it in all its churches, the program develops better. Acceptance and approval insure a good continuance.

When a denomination or mission does not fully accept a program, time and circumstance may lead to its dissolution. One missionary had a TEE program going before furlough, but when he returned he found the church had dropped it. While the church may need to staff the program after a short while, they may also need to fund it. If the denomination/mission is wholeheartedly behind it, the program has a solid base.

Future Prospects

Seventy-seven percent of administrators polled rate the future prospects of TEE as good. Their reasons vary, but essentially break down into six categories: growing programs, great leadership needs, method conducive to learning level, support of churches, educational philosophy, and significant volunteer participation. The future prospects are related to the signals of success given previously but represent the future orientation of TEE.

Growing Programs

Pochi, former director of COCIN—the largest TEE program in Africa— says, "Despite inflation many more people are joining TEE. Several churches are today starting TEE programs while others are making inquiries about how to start one" (1990q). Others also point to growing interest and "increasing numbers interested in the program." The future prospects look good because of widening interest.

Hartwig Harms of Mekane Yesus Seminary in Ethiopia affirms that because the churches of Africa are growing, "residential training cannot supply enough workers" (MYS 1990q). The prospects for TEE look good because growing churches will necessitate more programs.

Bill Mercer in Mozambique reports, "We are now branching out into the provinces. To date, acceptance has been good" (EBADM 1990q). Expansion into new areas makes for positive prospects.

Clearly, many administrators have good reason to see a promising future on the basis of expanding and potential new programs.

Great Leadership Training Needs

Churches in Africa are growing at a fast rate. Residential schools cannot meet all the leadership training needs. More kinds of training like TEE will be employed to develop an optimum number of leaders. Hunger for learning abounds. A growing desire for training is evident even among African Independent Churches. International Christian Ministries (ICM) in Kenya says that they have set a goal to help the African Independent Churches (AICs) in their leadership training. If a growing church is to be given good direction, training needs will have to be addressed.

Leadership training needs are also becoming apparent among the post-secondary (college age and young adult) population of many African countries. ICM, COCIN, and others are attempting higher level TEE to meet the leadership training demands on the higher educational level. Only a small percentage of high school graduates go on to Bible College and seminary, and yet many well-educated young adults are very active in leadership positions in churches. TEE will play a major role in their training.

All over Africa distances impede the delivery of good leadership development programs. Erickson of the Baptist Evangelical Association in Ethiopia says, "For our needs (even with new freedoms) it will be some time before we have adequate, trained leadership for . . . churches, scattered across vast, often isolated terrain" (BEATEE 1990q). TEE, in part a form of distance education, can play an important role.

A big market for leadership training challenges the churches and missions of Africa. Administrators perceive that great leadership needs demand extension training.

Method Conducive to Learning Level

Many of the TEE programs are using the AEAM series of programmed texts edited by Fred and Grace Holland and published by Evangel Press in Nairobi, Kenya. While the use of these texts by TEE programs is not required, they are meeting immediate needs on a basic educational level.

Steven Hardy, an AEF missionary says, "These studies are written at a level where our people currently are" (IBE 1990q). Jim Lo of the Wesleyan TEE program in Zimbabwe and South Africa says, "I feel that the method of teaching TEE offers is conducive to the learning styles of the Africans. What the churches in Africa need is discipling. TEE offers this to the churches" (EWBSE 1990q).

Often, a TEE program is the only Bible education and training a church may offer. In fact, PEDIM in Burkina Faso is "using it as a required program for local church leaders" (1990q). Phumelela Extension Bible School of the Alliance Church in South Africa (with over 600 students) requires it of all their leaders. While some have to reorganize their program because of too rapid expansion (see case study, chapter seven) and others must sell it to pastors, many have seen the blessing and find it just fits the learning level of their leaders.

Support of the Churches

I was surprised to see that acceptance by the churches was a reason given for good future prospects. PEDIM leaders in Burkina Faso say, "The church has begun to appreciate this new (to them) program" (1990q). Another leader reports that the reason for good future prospects is that the church desires extension.

In Lesotho, Dick Dunkerton is training one hundred Sotho evangelists using TEE. "The program has the full support of the director of the Bible School and Seminary as well as the executive committee of the Lesotho Evangelical Church" (MTS 1990q). What Dunkerton is doing is needed all over Africa—he is bringing leadership training to those who cannot get it in other ways. And he has the backing of the church.

Church leaders desire that leadership training be related to the church. Kenya Assemblies of God Extension Bible School (KAGE) indicates that this is a reason they think the prospects are good. "It is one means of keeping our training related to the church" (1990q). KAGE requires that every pastor go through all twenty-four TEE books before graduating with a diploma. A church based TEE program has good future prospects.

Educational Philosophy

Referring to the praxis nature of TEE, one administrator plainly states that TEE's future is bright because all educational philosophies are moving in that direction. All education, including residential, is taking more cognizance of the practical outworking of learning and reflection. Pure "intellectual" learning is being challenged. More and more educators prefer and use practical application.

Peter Gunning in South Africa is doing a thesis on TEE as a path to critical consciousness. He says, "(TEE is) the only way to go in our context" (SJBES 1990q). In the context of change where dialogue and discussion are givens for democracy, TEE can be a real force for helping people to think and express themselves.

Volunteer Teachers

The leader for the TEE program of the Baptist Theological Seminary in Zimbabwe observes that significant interest and "participation...on the part of volunteer teachers (class leaders)," give reason to be optimistic (1990q). I have seen firsthand the work of volunteer TEE class leaders and would concur that to a large degree the future of TEE is in their hands.

So important is the volunteer discussion group leader (tutor) that Thornton put together a course guide designed specifically for group leaders (1990). The book grew out of a course for TEE enablers at Daystar University College in Nairobi, July 4-5, 1988 where seventeen key TEE leaders gathered. In the opening of the book she writes,

> The TEE group leader can make TEE a joyful learning experience, or a series of dutifully spent hours without tangible results. Unless the group leader has a thorough understanding of his or her role and has got clear guide-lines on how to lead a group, he or she may fail. (1990, 1)

Voluntary participation comprises part of the spiritual foundation of TEE (Thornton 1990, 13) and is surely a key ingredient of its future. But seven out of thirty administrators were not as optimistic as to the future of TEE.

Cautions on the Future

While seventy-seven percent of administrators rate the future prospects of TEE as good, that leaves twenty-three percent who are not as optimistic about its future.

An experienced Baptist TEE leader in Malawi says, "Unless the economies of Africa change, anything requiring paper, pens, and ink will not reach the masses" (BTEEM 1990q). This cautions us against overoptimism. Many African countries are in debt. Runaway inflation is hurting Zaire, Zambia, Malawi, and many other African countries. A missionary in Zaire comments, "Given the economic situation in Zaire, I don't see TEE ever being able to function without outside help, especially financial" (CECA-ETE 1990q).

Finances are a critical factor when considering the future of TEE. Missions and churches cannot afford to cut off support to TEE leaders or deprive them of office space if they expect them to keep programs going. Funds for effective administration and supervision are necessary to its future prospects.

Another aspect of finances, often overlooked, is that some students pay their fees late (or not at all). Yet TEE as a program is dependent on prompt payment of fees so books can be purchased for the next term. When TEE tutors do not collect the fees, there are problems. Good systems of strict administration will have to be devised for payment of fees.

Another problem affecting TEE's future is the transmission of those fees which are collected into the right accounts. If money is missing or unaccounted for, indications are that either the system or moral fibre is not working as it should. Sometimes students ask for books and do not pay. Sometimes students pay but somehow the money does not reach headquarters. Both problems must be addressed if the future is to be brighter than the past. Otherwise financial limitations will limit TEE.

One administrator feels the future prospects of TEE are not good because:

> We don't have funds now which would permit us to maintain the present TEE program by developing a stock of TEE materials and enable us to grow significantly. About 99% of our budget comes from overseas churches. (CECA-ETE 1990q)

The main reason given for a cautious outlook on TEE is lack of financing. The future of TEE programs which lack effective financing stands in jeopardy.

In the next chapter, I turn to data resulting from a closed questionnaire (number 2—Appendix D) never before published.

CHAPTER FIVE

Figures and Percentages

George Foxall of ACTEA has been gathering statistics on TEE programs in Africa, listing 158 spread across 32 countries. He has data on one hundred of these, revealing that they range from small programs to those which are truly large. He explains,

> Currently, ACTEA has 158 TEE programmes listed in its files with data on 100 (63%) in 32 countries in Africa. Normally each national church organization has a central TEE office and it is listed as a single programme. However, a number of church denominations operate regional programmes and these are listed separately...Consequently, the term 'TEE program' may mean in some instances a single small local programme of less than five students, or in another case a multi-centered programme with over three thousand students. (1991, 2)

I sent a lengthy closed questionnaire containing 77 questions (see Appendix D) to the administrators of all 158 TEE programs. From this group 78 responded, about 50%. The number of TEE programs is always fluid: new ones spring up; a few programs have several different names (one has four names); a few other programs have become defunct and no longer exist; and poor mail service took its toll so that in some cases administrators never received the questionnaire. Therefore, the response may actually be higher than 50%.

Programs which replied to my questionnaire were those with a definite administrative base and a *network* of classes (not just a single class), and all were organized well enough to answer the 77 questions. Each question was limited in response range from three to five choices.

The sample was well spread out across the continent in four regions south of the Sahara: West Africa 35%, East Africa 26%, Central Africa 15% and Southern Africa 24%. In addition, responses came from 22 out of the 32 African countries which Foxall reports as having TEE programs. Such a spread contributes to the representative nature of the sample.

The data gathered not only contributes to the quantitative knowledge on TEE programs in Africa, but is used to enhance the qualitative description of the case studies in chapters six to ten.

Information gathered from the questionnaires (chapters four and five) are compared with findings in the case studies (chapters six to ten) to develop a summary picture (chapters eleven and twelve) and help answer the question, "What makes TEE effective?"

Table of Longevity

In answer to the question, "How long has your program been in operation?" the following responses were given:

Table 5.1

AGE OF PROGRAM	Number	Percent (n=77)
0-3 Years	12	16%
4-6 Years	14	18%
7-10 Years	18	23%
11-13 Years	10	13%
14-17 Years	15	20%
18-20 Years	7	9%
Above 21 Years	1	1%

The average TEE program in Africa has been in existence between 7 and 14 years. 18 fall right on the mean (between 7 and 10 years). Nearly 60% are under 10 years old, while 10% are 18 years or above.

This study confirms Foxall's data regarding the youthfulness of African TEE when he states that 59% of the programs were established in the 1980s, but only 38% in the 1970s (1991, 3).

Two inferences may be drawn from the relative newness of the programs: firstly, it is difficult to trace historical trends because they have not had much time to develop; secondly, African leaders themselves are still absorbing the concept of TEE and how programs are helping the church. Data for evaluation must be carefully gathered.

Primary Aims of TEE

"What was the original and primary aim of your TEE program?" Responses are arranged in rank order from highest to lowest percentage in the "Yes" column.

Table 5.2

Percent

PRIMARY AIMS	No	Somewhat	Yes
Train Lay Leaders (n=72)	3	15	82
Teach the Bible (n=67)	1	36	63
Develop Disciples (n=61)	7	39	54
Develop Character (n=57)	5	42	53
Develop Pastoral Skills (n=63)	7	41	52

Notice that a different number (n) responded to each Primary Aim. Those who did not respond to each item may have thought only a few responses were necessary. An overwhelming 82% felt strongly enough about the training of lay leaders to check "Yes" as a primary aim in their TEE program. Clearly, the training of the *whole body*, not just pastors, is in view here. Development of pastoral skills is not as prominent as lay training, receiving 52% of "Yes" responses. Pastoral training does stand as a valued objective, but development of unordained people predominates in African TEE programs.

Criteria of Success

The question, "What criteria of success or effectiveness would you use for your program?" is focused on student activity. Responses are listed in rank order according to percentage under "Very Much."

Table 5.3

Percent

CRITERIA	Not	Somewhat	Very Much
Works in the Church (n=72)	1	28	71
Completes Book (n=67)	1	33	66
Spiritual Maturation (n=67)	0	36	64
Attends Classes (n=63)	5	36	59
Witnesses (n=66)	0	47	53
Helps Pastor (n=62)	2	60	38
Solves Problems (n=57)	5	77	18

In choosing the criteria relating to student activity by which administrators would consider their program successful, 71% said the highest criterion was that their students work in the church.

The second choice, "completes the book," is understandable. The course requires that the book be completed, a task demanding faithfulness in study over a period of time. If students are not completing the books, the program is not challenging them and sustaining their interest. If they are, something is going right in that program. Therefore completing books will likely be chosen as a criterion for success.

But more than that, the administrator considers whether or not his students are working in the church. The fact that students work in the church comprises the barometer of success for TEE programs in Africa. One of the original intents of TEE at its inception was that natural leaders be trained in their church context. Results show that effective extension programs are indeed linked with church work.

Are Aims Fulfilled

The question, "To what degree are the aims of your TEE program being fulfilled?" elicited the following results.

Table 5.4

DEGREE OF FULFILLMENT	Number	Percent (n=76)
Not at All	5	7
Somewhat	19	25
Uncertain	3	4
Being Fulfilled	42	55
Greatly Fulfilled	7	9

To the degree that program aims are fulfilled, effectiveness can be measured. The above chart reveals a very positive picture of how administrators view their programs. 64% reported that their goals are either "Being Fulfilled" (55%) or are "Greatly Fulfilled" (9%). 25% feel that their program goals are only "Somewhat" fulfilled. 7% clearly feel that their goals are "Not at All" fulfilled. This variable shows that the great majority of TEE administrators feel that their programs are attaining the goals they have set.

Toward the end of the questionnaire, I used a verifying inquiry, similar to the one above, to run a check on the response: "Do you think that the original aim(s) of your program are being fulfilled?" Here are the results:

Table 5.5

DEGREE OF FULFILLMENT	Number	Percent
No (not fulfilled)	4	5
Somewhat	35	46
Yes (being done)	28	37
Very Much So	9	12

When asked in this format, only 37% indicate that their programs are being fulfilled ("Yes"), whereas in the first question on aims 55% claimed their programs were "Being Fulfilled." The category "Somewhat" in the second question has much higher percentage (46%) than the earlier question (25%). Note that 12% answered that their aims were "Very Much So" fulfilled, better than the 9% of the earlier variable, "Greatly Fulfilled."

The results of the first chart are verified by the second, but slightly mitigated in that more say their programs are "Somewhat" fulfilled as over against "Being Fulfilled." In Table #4, 80% feel that their program aims are "Somewhat" and "Being Fulfilled" while 7% are "Not at All" fulfilled. In Table #5, 83% are "Somewhat" and "Yes" fulfilled versus 5% "No," not fulfilled. The combined results of the three positive categories are: in Table #4, 89% positive versus 7% "Not at All" and in Table #5, 95% positive versus 5% "No." Exact response categories in both tables would have improved measurement.

Although there is no meaningful difference between the two tables, why is there any difference? Did the administrators think more analytically about their program after working through the questionnaire (Table 5.5 came near the end of Questionnaire 2; Table 5.4 at the beginning)? Did the actual exercise of doing the questionnaire help them think more deeply about their programs? Did the respondents think of current aims in Table #4 but original aims in Table #5? Further research could clarify the issue.

Missionary or National Leadership

Is there any correlation between the opinion of administrators on their program's fulfillment and whether or not that particular administrator is a national or a missionary? Would a national administrator report differently than a missionary? To discover this I first had to determine the number of national and missionary administrators reporting. Note that in the following table, 58% of programs were headed by missionaries and 42% by nationals.

Table 5.6

CHIEF ADMINISTRATOR   Number   Percent (n=77)

	Number	Percent
Missionary	45	58
National	32	42

Foxall claims that African staff are leading the majority of TEE programs in Africa. He says, "In the overall picture there is a steady positive transition from expatriate control to African administration in TEE in Africa" (1991, 6). While I concur that there certainly is a continuing and positive transition, the responses to my administrators questionnaire show a different picture in regard to the chief administrator. Being acquainted with Foxall's questionnaire, I would say that there may have been room for overlap in his categories. For instance, he makes no difference between head administration and teachers. In my questionnaire, only the chief administrator was requested to fill it out.

The following scale shows the correlation between answers from national and missionary administrators on degree of program fulfillment.

Table 5.7

DEGREE OF FULFILLMENT	Percent Missionary	Percent National (n=76)
Not at All	5	9
Somewhat	32	16
Uncertain	2	6
Being Fulfilled	52	59
Greatly Fulfilled	9	10

37% of missionary administrators judge their programs as "Somewhat" or "Not at All" fulfilled; whereas 25% of national administrators chose these categories. Missionary administrators may be somewhat more critical of their programs than nationals.

As to the higher categories, "Being Fulfilled" and "Greatly Fulfilled," 61% of missionaries and 69% of nationals indicate positive fulfillment of their programs. From Chi-square, Pearson "r", and Spearman R tests, no significant correlation exits between degree of fulfillment and whether a national or missionary administrator filled out the questionnaire. This lack of correlation indicates that not only do missionary administrators evaluate TEE as fulfilling its aims, but national administrators also see TEE programs as effective. Both missionaries and nationals report similarly that their programs are being fulfilled.

Accreditation

TEE administrators were asked to "indicate if you are accredited from an academic institution."

Table 5.8

ACCREDITED FROM INSTITUTION	Number	Percent
Yes	33	43
Other	6	6
No	39	51

Half of the TEE programs reporting are not accredited by an academic institution. This means that academic accreditation does not appear to be a major controlling factor for many of the programs. I interpret the lack of formal accreditation as meaning that the extension program will go on with or without academic backing. It also reveals that TEE can exist as a church based program away from an institution. Therefore the programs may be formal or nonformal.

TEE's battle for equivalence with residence requirements may be reflected here. Perhaps accreditation is not readily available. ACTEA has an accreditation process for TEE, so we may see more programs gaining accreditation. Turley suggests that a strong link be make with residence programs (1991a, 44–47).

TEE has the priority of functional leadership and demands a different way of looking at accreditation. Certainly the nonformal nature of extension training is revealed in the above percentages. Although nearly 100% of the programs give grades and certificates, over half are not linked with an academic institution for accreditation. Ferris has given a list of pertinent criteria for TEE accreditation standards (1986) which focus on values that go beyond traditional thinking, pertinent for functional leadership.

Helping the Church

The positive answers to the question, "Do you see evidence that your TEE students are helping their local churches to grow?" denote a major value administrators have seen in extension.

Table 5.9

HELPING THE CHURCH	Number	Percent (n=77)
No, They are Not	0	0
Uncertain	10	13
Sometimes	19	25
Yes, They are	48	62

87% report that their students do help their churches, either "Sometimes" (25%) or "Yes, They are" (62%).

The following chart shows exactly how they are helping. It ranks student activity according to cumulative percentages. The "Cumulative" column is comprised of the "Sometimes" and "Always" values.

Table 5.10

Percent

HELPING ACTIVITY	Never	Seldom	Sometimes	Always	Cum%
Teach/Preach	2	4	63	31	94
Lead Services	1	7	56	36	92
Witness	1	9	63	27	90
Bring People in	1	9	79	10	89
Help People	3	11	72	14	86
Stop Fights (Quarrels)	8	46	36	10	46

These figures affirm the reality—that the overwhelming majority of TEE students are involved in church work. Foxall notes this when he presents the preliminary finding that

Though data is far from a complete picture of the church in Africa,...at least...59 TEE programmes are serving national churches of over 32,000 congregations with an average Sunday morning attendance of nearly seven million people. (1991, 6–7)

Problems

Numerous problems confront TEE in Africa. Some of these problems are so overwhelming that programs fizzle out. It is difficult to find out which programs have become defunct and why. The problems listed below, however, if left unattended and not overcome would surely paralyze an extension program. TEE contains complexities of operation and demands alert leadership to tackle these problems. They are listed in rank order under the "Always" column.

Table 5.11

Percent

PROBLEMS RANKED	Never	Sometimes	Always
Lack of Funding	26	57	17
Lack of Teacher Transp.	38	48	14
Lack of Books	27	60	13
Lack of Administrators	41	48	11
Lack of Church Support	25	65	10
Untrained Tutors	35	58	7
Not Paying Fees	21	75	4
Not Keeping Attendance	41	55	4
Unable to Do Books	40	56	4
Students Lack Motivation	28	70	2
No Place to Meet	90	10	0

The category "Sometimes" is rather vague, and administrators tend to that value if unsure. If something is "Always" a problem, it must be taken as highly significant. In rank order the most indicative of these are lack of funding, lack of teacher transport, lack of books, lack of administrators, and lack of church support.

Looking at the "Sometimes" column, note that 75% sometimes have a problem with payment of fees. This reflects the general economic situation in Africa where extremely low incomes are prevalent in many countries. Only 4% say it is *always* a problem, indicative of the fact that students attempt to pay the fees in spite of hardships.

Noting the other high percentages in the "Sometimes" column, 70% are reported as poorly motivated. This response is difficult to interpret because most TEE students work in the church and complete the books, thereby showing motivation. The "Sometimes" value is too broad a category. It may be that an administrator, looking over his program, thinks of those few students in his entire program who lack motivation. He therefore checks "Sometimes," because it is not a case of "Never" having unmotivated students. 28% do report that they never have poorly motivated students. Further research on this question should be done with special attention to indicators of students who lack motivation.

Although 65% say they "Sometimes" have a problem with church support, 25% "Never" have a problem with it. Just about an equal number have no problem with funding. This finding should be further studied and may suggest that one secret of solving the funding problem is to gain the support of the church.

Students and Evangelism

The following chart records the kind of evangelism done by TEE students. The question to the administrators was, " How are your students linked with an evangelistic program in your local church?"

Table 5.12

Percent (n=72)

KIND OF EVANGELISM Not Sure Seldom Sometimes Always

	Not Sure	Seldom	Sometimes	Always
Evangelize on Their Own	3	6	67	24
Evangelize with Pastor	10	17	64	9
Evangelize in Teams	12	25	57	6

When asked whether students evangelize on their own, the answers "Sometimes" (67%) and "Always" (24%) predominate over "Not sure" (3%) and "Seldom" (6%). Evangelizing on their own gives an extremely high 91% cumulative total. Apparently evangelism is the life style of the greater majority of TEE students. While students evangelize with their pastor and, to a lesser degree, in teams, personal witness received the higher percentages.

The preponderance of personal evangelism is in agreement with the results of a study done in Kenya by Daystar College where 87% of both urban and rural students (n=98) said their TEE study has helped them lead someone to the Lord (Urbanization 1990, 6).

Effective service in evangelism surfaces as an expression of student devotion to Christ and gauges the health of a TEE program.

Students and Skills

It is possible to study the Bible by means of rote memory only. Is that the case in TEE, or are ministry skills also being developed? The following table indicates the answers to the question, "What skills are your students developing through your TEE program?" Responses are in rank order under "Many."

Table 5.13

Percent

STUDENT SKILLS	None	Some	Many
Study the Bible	1	29	70
Pray	1	34	65
Preach	0	43	57
Witness	1	49	50
Lead Bible Study	2	62	36
Lead Worship	3	61	36
Counsel	12	79	9

70% of programs report that "Many" of their students develop Bible study skills. This tops the list. Foxall says 80% of TEE programs use the AEAM Text-Africa material (1991, 5). Note, then, that this material promotes Bible study skills. Development in prayer, preaching, and witnessing follow in next higher percentages. The extreme "Many" column is of importance because of the restricted range of the values and the assumption that more would tend toward "Some", a midpoint, rather than to the extreme. Yet the "Many" column was often deliberately chosen.

Cumulative totals of the "Some" and "Many" columns provide amazingly high percentages. This highlights the fact that TEE is a vehicle through which Christians can express their gifts, finding training, development, occasion, and opportunity. Spiritually oriented skills are being developed.

Helping the Pastor

Helping the pastor is another category used to determine skills being developed by TEE students. The question was, "How do students help their pastor outside of class?" Responses are ranked according to the "Always" column.

Table 5.14

Percent

ASSISTING PASTOR	Never	Sometimes	Always
Lead Worship (n=68)	0	68	32
Witness (n=66)	0	79	21
Visit the Sick (n=62)	0	79	21
Bring Others (n=61)	2	82	16
Counsel Sorrowing (57)	4	81	15
Visit Members (60)	7	83	10

Interestingly, extension students help their pastors most by leading services. Yet skills are rarely taught in TEE seminars specifically in the area of leading church services. Students stir up their desire to serve, and leading services is frequently opened to them. The specifics are modeled by the pastor—what to do and in what order.

Note that if cumulative percentages ("Sometimes" and "Always") of witnessing and visiting the sick are calculated, 100% of extension students do something in these areas. Giving counsel to the sorrowing and visitation of members are last on the list. Counseling stands low on all lists. Self-study material needs to be written and skills taught to develop students in this area.

Tutors and Discussion Seminars

Answering the question, "What do *others* report about your discussion group leaders when they lead their classes?" the following summary gives helpful information. Note that the "Sometimes" and "Always" columns are added together to create the "Cumulative %" column.

Table 5.15

Percent

TUTOR SKILLS	Never	Sometimes	Always	Cum%
Begin with Prayer (n=60)	0	7	93	100
Get Others to Talk (n=61)	3	49	48	97
Give Quizzes (n=57)	10	46	44	90
Review at End (n=55)	13	54	33	87
Help Solve Problems (n=58)	3	74	23	97
Talk Most Often (n=59)	7	74	19	93
Repeat the Lesson(n=51)	l6	68	16	84

In TEE training workshops, tutors are taught how to conduct seminars and are given minimal basic instruction on how to lead a discussion. Group dynamics are touched upon, but not given the emphasis required by the importance of this skill. The above table reflects the basic variables necessary for a tutor. For example, all tutors are taught to begin the class with prayer. 93% always do this. But they are also taught to get others to talk. Yet only 48% always do this. Again they are taught not to talk very much, but 19% always talk too much. The obvious need of further training is exposed by this frequency check.

When we combine the "Somewhat" and "Always" columns, we find that 97% get others to talk, while 93% do most of the talking. This is an interesting anomaly. Administrators who get feedback on tutors who are talking too much in class may check that category in the "Sometimes-Always" columns, while at the same time recording that the talkative tutor does get others in the class to talk as well. This does not define how much talking is done by the tutors and how much by the class. It does indicate that these tutors, even if they do provoke some class discussion, are in general taking more time than they should away from discussion in order to talk themselves.

A sociogram which plots group interaction is needed to determine how much each tutor and participant actually talks. Follow-up training seminars would further hone the skills of tutors.

Discussion Seminar Activity

The following table reveals the results of two questions phrased in this way: "Do your discussion group leaders report that they are doing problem solving in class?" and "...that there is good interaction between the students?"

Table 5.16

Percent

SEMINAR ACTIVITY	No	Uncertain	Yes
Problem Solving Going on (n=68)	7	27	66
Good Student Interaction (n=68)	3	15	82

The first question asks for an assessment regarding problem solving in class. Is it being done? 66% respond "Yes", indicative of the fact that problem solving is done in many TEE classes. In the second question, 82% report good interaction between students.

While these percentages look good, further research is necessary for an in-depth perspective. Baird and Weinberg suggest several sociograms which help relate the kinds of interaction going on within a discussion group (1991, 233–282). These sociograms include a diagram of the seating arrangement of the discussion class, tell who is talking to whom and how many times participants (including the leader) speak. Baird and Weinberg also give lists of detailed questions which help determine details of the type and tone of responses.

Qualifications of Seminar Leaders

The qualifications of discussion seminar leaders are so important I included several questions in this regard. The point of departure for any training is often the entry qualifications of those who lead. If they lack Bible background or understanding of the TEE model, their performance will be weak.

How do seminar leaders stack up? The listing below is on the values "Never," "Sometimes," and "Often." I included the cumulative percentages of "Sometimes" and "Often" in a final column, coming up with the following rank order:

Table 5.17

Percent

BACKGROUND OF TUTOR	Never	Sometimes	Often	Cum%
Pastors, TEE Experience	8	54	38	92
Bible School Graduates, TEE Experience	14	43	43	86
Bible School Graduates, No TEE Experience	27	61	12	73
TEE Students, No Bible School	32	50	18	68
Pastors, No TEE Experience	32	61	7	68

Under the "Often" category, Bible school graduates with TEE experience (TEE methodology is now taught in Bible schools) are used as leaders in 43% of the cases, and pastors with TEE experience are used 38% of the time. These are shown to be the preferred leaders, the first choice of those available.

What amazes me is that so many pastors with no TEE experience (61%) and Bible school graduates with no TEE experience (again 61%) are "Sometimes" used to lead TEE classes. Even considering the novelty of TEE, with most programs between seven and fourteen years old, this use of so many apparently untrained leaders probably does harm to the programs, and again demonstrates the desperate need for trained and qualified tutors.

A cumulative 68% "Sometimes" or "Often" use TEE students with no Bible school training. In my experience mature TEE students do make good tutors in many cases, because they teach as they have been taught—by discussion. This presumes the tutor has completed sufficient courses over many years to qualify in the area of Bible knowledge. A broad base of Bible knowledge makes the tutor better qualified as a resource person.

All of this further reflects TEE's rapid expansion, drawing in and using all who could be available as tutors as soon as possible. Enthusiasm and rapid expansion needs to be tempered with wise planning and adequate training.

Tutor Training

Types of training offered to tutors are displayed according to rank and percentage under "Often" in response to: "What kind of training does your TEE program provide for TEE discussion group leaders?"

Table 5.18

Percent

TYPE OF TRAINING	Never	Sometimes	Often (n=66)
Basic Training	6	27	67
Keep Interaction Going	10	40	50
Improve Questioning Ability	12	46	42
How to Solve Problems	13	49	38

While 67% of class leaders receive basic tutor training, which includes fundamentals on how to conduct classes, from personal experience I have observed that not much time is given in this training to the development of discussion facilitation. Only 50% "Often" received training in how to keep interaction going, yet student interaction is the heart of the TEE model.

Note also that only 42% "Often" had training in how to ask discussion-provoking questions. Questioning ability stands as the essence of a good group discussion leader. Unless we develop this side of the facilitator-catalyst model, there is minimal chance of stimulating meaningful class discussion. A much smaller percentage had training in learning to help solve problems in class; yet this is the facet of TEE that makes it so different from theoretical learning which uses hypothetical situations. The tutor should attempt to help the participants attack real problems, and through interaction devise solutions consis-

tent with Scripture. Here indeed is a skill which must be developed for
extension to reach its potential in leadership development.

In this connection, I also wanted to know "How many training
sessions have you held for your discussion group leaders this calendar
year and last calendar year?"

Table 5.19

TRAINING SESSIONS REPORTED (n=78)	Percent in 1991	Percent in 1990
None	45	42
One	36	28
Two	8	9
Three	3	10
Four	1	4
Five	3	0
Six	1	1
Nine	3	0
Ten	0	3
Sixteen up	0	3

Totalling the percentages, we find that only 55% reported holding
training sessions in 1991; only 58% in 1990. This reveals a great lack of
training for tutors and does not bode well for TEE in Africa. Something
must be done to change this picture. The frequency table above is not
designed to correlate the number of training sessions with the general
effectiveness of the tutor.

Correlation of Basic Tutor Training
and Group Dynamics

Do training sessions correlate with discussion class performance? Does receiving basic training correlate with "Getting Others to Talk," a tutor skill (see Table #15) which is part of the group dynamics of discussion? The following table shows that the resultant relationship is not a chance finding.

Table 5.20

GROUP DYNAMICS IN CLASS   Basic Tutor Training

Group Dynamics in Class	Basic Tutor Training
Tutor Does Most of Talking	-.12
Tutor Gets Others to Talk	.33**
Tutor Repeats the Lesson	.04
Tutor Helps Solve Problems	-.02
Problem Solving Goes on	.26*
Student Interaction Goes on	.21

*p<.05 **p<.01

This cluster of group dynamics, "Tutor Gets Others to Talk," "Problem Solving Goes on," and "Student Interaction Goes on," means that wherever training is given it affects the performance of the tutors. Results would be even better statistically if more programs were given training sessions at least twice a year. It is a mystery how nearly half of TEE programs can function without an ongoing program of tutor training.

The correlation coefficient (Spearman R=.33p<.01) indicates that a modest but statistically significant relationship exists between basic tutor training and getting others to talk. In addition, there is a close though nonsignificant correlation between basic training and student interaction in class. The close correlation indicates that if training classes are increased the figure may become significant.

Although it is true that people may interact with one another to exchange opinions, a guided discussion which leads to problem solving demands certain skills.

Tutor training correlates well with problem solving in class. Coaching in this area goes along with increased problem solving among class members. The more a tutor is trained to allow problem solving to take place in class between students, the more this group dynamic occurs.

A negative correlation (although statistically insignificant) is obtained between basic tutor training and tutors talking too much in class. A negative correlation may mean an inverse relationship, and (if it is not by chance) is as it should be in this case. More tutor training should lead to less tutor talking, so the negative correlation is supportive of TEE theory. However, because of the frequency of tutors "Talking Most Often" (Table #15), this conclusion is tentative.

"Tutor Helps Solve Problems" (Table #20) is also a negative correlation. In TEE theory, problem solving is not done by the tutor. Tutors lead students to solve their own problems within a context of class interaction. This negative correlation could be by chance; nevertheless it does go along with TEE theory.

My hypothesis as a clear result of this study is that more specific and cogent training must be pursued if greater discussion class effectiveness is to be developed. Longitudinal studies are called for to determine future effectiveness. TEE is not a simple form of leadership development. It requires training in group dynamics not easily applied without extensive practice.

From a general survey of seventy-eight TEE programs, let us now turn our attention to five case studies for an in-depth look at how these programs work.

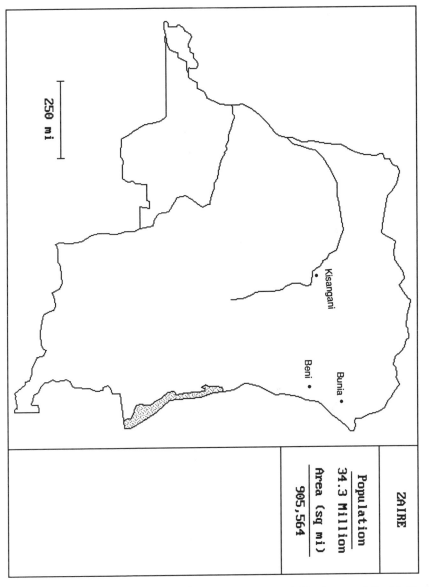

ZAIRE

Population
34.3 Million
Area (sq mi)
905,564

250 mi

Kisangani •

Beni •

Bunia •

CHAPTER SIX

From Bunia to Beni

My first case study comes from the African Inland Mission's daughter church in Zaire. It incorporates a widespread program of 150 centers with 50 monitors or discussion group leaders. The program is called in French "Enseignement Theologique par Extension" (ETE) of the "Communaute Evangelique au Centre de l'Afrique" (CECA), and it began in 1975. At first it was advertised as equivalent to the residence program—twelve books equalling one year.

Soon, however it was realized that while a four-year program required 48 books, both writing and translation lagged far behind that. Only 18 books of the AEAM Text-Africa series have been translated into Swahili. Equivalence faded into the background, and they began to concentrate on a functional mode: developing leaders in the local congregations such as catechists, evangelists, elders, deacons, youth, and children's leaders.

The national director of this program, Kana Muzuro Way, wrote, "Some years ago, the church (CECA) in which I am involved began to grow in number. So many local congregations were created, but there were few leaders in the church who were trained in Bible school" (Way 1985, 6). This tells the story, common in Africa, of the need for practical local church leadership programs. Bible schools did not produce enough leaders, and most of the leaders had not received any Bible training. The TEE program was begun to meet the need for leadership development in the local church.

Aim of the Program

The ETE (TEE) program in Zaire is a bona fide church program, recognized along with all other Christian Education efforts being promoted by CECA. Early in its history its goals were separate from that of the Bible Schools, the aim being the edification and training of those already involved in ministry, and eventually all Christians. Both pastors and laypeople attend.

Missionaries, pastors, and TEE coordinators alike testify that the program gives opportunity for the people to get training if they cannot go to Bible school. TEE "offers a mobile program of study that allows lay leaders in outlying communities to get additional training without leaving their present church responsibilities" (Barnett 1991, 5). The program helps Christians to mature and trains lay leaders, elders, deacons, and Sunday school teachers for the church. Besides giving biblical knowledge, the program aims to "increase Christian commitment. We encourage our audience to share their faith with others, to witness effectively..." (Way 1985, 7).

Administration

The program is widely spread over eight provinces in one of the largest church communities in northeastern Zaire. It is not attached to a school or institute but is associated with the Bible training department of CECA.

The head of the program, called the director, has six regional coordinators (presidents), either a key national or a missionary, under him—one for each province. The province is naturally divided by the geography of the area into sections loosely organized and responsible to the regional coordinator, who in turn works under the director.

A church or group of churches holding TEE classes is called a center. A pastor who is qualified to lead a center may start several classes locally and send reports to the regional coordinator, who is responsible for administration in his region. This fits the decentralized, rural pattern of TEE in Africa: "A network of centers extending out from the administrative center of the programme and being visited by full-time (or part-time) staff members" (Hogarth, Gatimu and Barrett 1983, 75).

The national director pointed out to me the value of the regional coordinators. They secure records, do training seminars for the tutors, send in reports to the director, and help him keep abreast of the situation in each region. He showed me a list sent to him by a regional coordinator of new class leaders being trained in Todro, a district where TEE is flourishing. The director of CECA-ETE has a central office, but his work as encourager, instructor, and problem solver, frequently takes him out to the distant regions.

CECA's TEE program began as a separate program parallel to the eight Bible schools run by the mission and church. In one area, the regional coordinator has attempted to associate the program more closely with the Bible school. All TEE administration, student records, and grades in that district are done through the district Bible school, and the Bible school director helps oversee TEE. I interviewed the French-speaking Bible school director and found him thoroughly knowledgeable regarding book inventory and procedures class leaders use to start new courses. He showed me detailed files of grades, student practical work, and the courses each class had completed. A mobile library with a small supply of books is made available for TEE.

Component Parts: Praxis

Type of Students

Most of the students are mature people already involved in the church. Both men and women, married and single are trained. Language groups involved are Bangala, Swahili, and Pazande.

A church leader in Beni specified that TEE trains catechists to be pastors in the local churches, especially those who have not gone beyond primary school and do not have an adequate educational standard. They are out there in the rural areas doing the work, but academically are not qualified to enter our Bible schools. TEE teaches them to study God's Word. Also, some others have very large families which they would not be able to leave in order to go to Bible School. They profit by the TEE program.

The stress is on the fact that the local people are being trained. As one man proudly said, "I know several of them that have studied. Some have studied for a long time. Araho began Bible study and now he's a pastor. And Ranieko also. They all studied, they're just local people. They're people from our area."

Self-Study Material

CECA mostly uses the AEAM Text-Africa programmed books. Students like the books and say "they are important; the books give the main teaching and the class reinforces what we learn in the book. The book also provides homework, like asking us to prepare a message."

A pastor remarked on the relevancy of the books to Africa because they use African situations and names for people. He deeply appreciated the way the AEAM Text-Africa series is contextualized.

There is a problem with finding enough books to keep the program going. The national director says that "some years ago the program was really growing, but now we don't have enough books to run the program. In the Bangala region we do not have classes because we don't have enough books."

There are several reasons for this. One is that translation is a slow process. One missionary has prepared workbooks on individual Bible book studies for use in his classes because of a lack of translated books.

Another problem is the cost. Devaluation of currency combined with Zaire's run-away inflation prevent some from buying the books. Originally CECA-ETE brought in Swahili books from Kenya because they found it cheaper than producing them. Now, because of inflation, it has become expensive to bring them in from Kenya because of sizable customs costs.

Subsidy is needed. The program is selling the books at a loss, but the church is not able to support the program with a sufficient subsidy to solve the problem. Some students sell vegetables to buy their books.

I accompanied the director to find a former TEE student who was on his way to conduct a funeral. We bumped along a dirt road which petered out into a walking path. We walked along the road till, providentially, we met him near the place where mourners had gathered.

He told us that the books were very, very helpful, and aided him a lot in his pastoral work. He particularly referred to *Christian Family Living* (Conn and Simbiri 1978) as a text which taught him how to keep his family "in the face of life." He felt the books on the life of Christ should be studied first, and that pictures of various scenes would enhance the books. As for himself, he particularly wanted a chance to study *The Shepherd and His Work* (Crider and Msweli 1974). When I asked him why he was not studying, he said the books were unavailable.

Service in the Church

The director made it clear that TEE is helping Christians grow in grace and serve the Lord. It makes them thirsty for more study of the Word of God. Some have become preachers, others teach Sunday School, and most do some kind of work in the church.

One student told me that TEE has built him up in God's Word, and he has begun to serve as a pastor, preparing sermons and visiting the people. Another student testified, "I did not know how to preach, to pray, to witness, (or) to lead others to Christ, but now I can do all that without fear" (CECA 1990q). Students are sent out to take care of other churches, and if there is a need in the local church, they can fill it.

A missionary coordinator pointed out that the lack of a homiletics course is a glaring weakness. This affects the way students write the sermons they are expected to prepare.

Discussion Seminars

I found Mika and his church people working to extend the floor of their mud and wattle church in Bunia. His feet were very muddy, but he was willing to sit down with me and talk about TEE and the nine courses he had already taken. He described the discussion class as a meeting where they check their answers and then share their views and experiences together. Understanding was improved through discussion.

In a class I attended, the rapport between the students, as well as with the instructor, was good. A pastor remarked that "discussion starts easily; we talk about various problems in the class. The leader begins with a general question and each student gives his or her thoughts." A student commented, "Students do most of the talking among themselves, but the teacher (tutor) is there to help in areas we don't understand."

One of the difficulties is that students with different educational backgrounds are in the same class. The level of discussion satisfies some, but not others.

For Rev. Ngadjo, learning by TEE was deeper than learning in the resident Bible school. He enjoyed the discussions, the sharing of experiences, and the testimonies in the group. The program helped him improve his ministry and enabled him to answer questions about sin and salvation, which he could not do before.

Another pastor reported that a mutually beneficial relationship exists between work and study. He saw the advantage in doing ministry while studying. His study improved his ministry, and when he contributed in class it was from practical experience. Praxis at its best!

Tutor/Monitor

Pastors are often used as monitors; it helps the whole church accept the program; otherwise the program might be seen as a threat to the church. The pastor can delegate the discussion-leader role if he is too busy. Pastoral presence indicates church approval.

Administrators pointed out that the success of the class depends on the tutor and how well he can pick up the needs of the people. One missionary leader told me he has seen some problematic discussions, because pastors, who often lead groups, tend to preach as they teach. Other tutors also tend to talk more than their students, and that is not good. One basis for this weakness is that tutors, already responsible in their local churches, are very busy and do not have enough time to carefully prepare for discussion.

After completing two or three TEE courses, a pastor can take a training seminar called "Formation," and then begin to lead classes. Bible school graduates who have taken a TEE seminar and training course at Bible school can lead TEE classes as soon as they begin their work.

Five new TEE classes have begun in the Beni area through pastors newly graduated from Bible school. This is encouraging to the regional coordinator, who has some pastors who don't want to teach, fearing they will not have answers to the questions of TEE students. One missionary coordinator has been doing three-day seminars around his district to help tutors develop skill in directing questions, and provide training in giving answers to oft asked questions. The tutor has to prepare questions for each lesson. They need this kind of help to become resource persons as well as group leaders.

Tutor Training

The quality of tutors is controlled by adhering to certain standards.

1. The tutor must be a graduate of a Bible school.

2. The tutor must have attended three TEE courses taught by a qualified teacher (tutor) or have taken the TEE course in Bible School.

3. The tutor must have attended a seminar on leading TEE classes, a week-long workshop in which potential tutors are trained in the use of self-study books and group discussion skills. They are taught how to compose discussion and exam questions.

4. The tutors begin to teach and are inspected by the director who may attend up to three sessions.

5. If the tutor passes observation, then he/she is given a teacher's certificate. Giving certificates is a means of keeping the program standards high; the teacher gains respect from having the certificate.

One pastor gave this unsolicited remark, "The greatest thing which the church has is the TEE training program."

Spiritual Foundation

If results among the students is any indication of the spiritual foundation of the CECA-ETE program, then it has a spiritual base.

1. They try to read the Bible more. One student said that he appreciated TEE because it forced him to spend time in the Word of God daily. He had greater understanding of many Bible passages.

2. They try to rectify their lives. A certain pastor had been in charge of a hospital. During his time of administration, money disappeared. Later while taking a TEE class, he made things right. Today he teaches TEE classes for others in several centers and is scrupulous in money matters.

3. They try to improve their family lives.

4. Many testify to changed lives which can only be attributed to the work of the Holy Spirit. One student reported that now that he was studying the Word, he could see certain errors he was making in his Christian walk. Students and center leaders are enthusiastic, claiming that the TEE studies have changed their lives.

The aims of greater Christian commitment and development of Christian character in the CECA program are integral to the spiritual base. If results like this accrue, they are indeed building on a solid spiritual foundation.

External Relationships

Community

Leaders of CECA's extension program assert that their students are always witnessing to others in the community. However, when asked if they evangelize on their own, they report "seldom." Instead evangelism is done more frequently with the pastor or in teams.

Church Approval

After a short initial conflict with residential schools, the purposes of the extension program were settled and its place assured. The church and the pastors have accepted it. The director claims that this is so in all the communities. Another leader asserts that the church is happy with the program because centers continue to function, which is conversely also evidence of the church's interest. A missionary leader concludes that there is increasing church acceptance because they "own" the program.

One of the church's greatest felt needs is a lack of workers. Because of rapid growth, church workers cannot meet the needs. This evident lack of workers puts stress on the church to prepare more leaders. According to director Kana Muzuro Way, TEE is helping to fill that need.

Positively, TEE's acceptance by the church is aided by the fact that it complements the work of the Bible schools. As one pastor suggested, "The program (TEE) helps very much to shoulder the work in the Bible schools. (What) the Bible school is not able to do, TEE is able to do. The church gains benefit from those who go to the Bible school and also from those who are trained through the ETE program. They complement each other."

Problems

Three major problems plague the CECA program: lack of TEE books, lack of funding, and lack of teacher transport.

Lack of Books

I frequently heard the cry for books while I was in Zaire. So often did I hear this that I had to rephrase an interview question, "*Besides* the lack of books, what are some of the problems in TEE?" The dearth of books prevents the program from progressing as it should. While rarely reporting a lack of trained tutors, lack of books appears under the "Always" column. In an interview in the Beni area a pastor who had access to books asked me, "Right now we have a supply of books at the Bible school. If they run out, is the program going to fall flat?" *The* problem is the availability of books.

Lack of Funding

Inflation is high and students run into the obstacle of paying fees. A common excuse for dropping out is that the books are too expensive. Some have waited a whole year until they could get the fees before being able to study again. A complaint is registered that the church is not "with" the students, because they are not included in the church budget. Some feel that the church should pay half the cost of the books, but the church says it is unable to do so.

The Church is in straits because it cannot afford the ministries it already has. Although church leaders are behind TEE, they do need to put the program higher in their budget.

While noting the need for more personnel in administration, a pastor in Beni asked, "Where is the salary going to come from?" In addition, attempting to get African writers into the program is important but-lacks funding. The most poignant statement I heard summarizes the problem: "The *financial burden* is one that I don't see the church ever being able to carry on its own. If TEE is to continue, it will need to be carried by gifts from elsewhere."

Lack of Teacher Transport

Distances are a real barrier for TEE tutors. With long, rutted roads from one village to the next, the TEE tutor needs transport. Given the economy of Zaire, a missionary leader flatly states that the church is dependent on Western funding. "With $5000-$7000 a year, we could have two fully paid administrators with motorbike transport." Bicycles are needed for class leaders.

Areas like Zandeland that need TEE are up against this problem. Without transport no one can lead classes in their area. While some tutors can walk to their classes, to get out to other students is a formidable project.

Transport for teachers is one of the problems checked under the "Always" column in the administrator's questionnaire.

Innovations

Doing something different can be a very good thing. CECA's TEE program is flexible and they are willing to utilize various educational methods within the TEE model: "TEE programs may include a variety of theological and doctrinal studies, Bible lessons, lectures and discussions, practical ministry assignments and other pastoral training seminars" (Barnett 1991, 5).

As an example, sometimes a special two-week TEE course on *The Shepherd and His Work* (Crider and Msweli, 1974) is held. In the morning students do the lessons (i.e., they fill in their programmed workbooks); in the afternoon there are long discussion sessions. This intensive resembles a crash course, and some monitors/tutors are developed from it.

Another important innovation is the attempt of a regional coordinator to equip tutors in three-day seminars to deal with especially difficult theological problems.

Evaluation

The TEE program develops skills, gives leaders greater confidence, gets them into their Bibles, and enables them to answer questions which they could not do before.

Skills and Confidence

While wishing for even more skills, the top ones listed are witnessing, preaching, studying the Bible, family living, and praying.

Testimonies already given in this case study exemplify these skills and the new confidence of many students in using them.

Bible Study

In agreement with the results of our questionnaire in the previous chapter, Bible study is high on the list of results of involvement in TEE programs. Testimonies abound to the effect that students spend time in the Word daily. One leader lists three activities related to Bible study which are evident to him:

1. Helping Christians develop a daily Bible study time
2. Helping pastors become teachers of the Word
3. Giving Christians an opportunity to study what they believe

Answering Questions

One of the most scintillating interviews I had was with a TEE student who said there are many kinds of questions in the cities, and studying through TEE gave him the ability to answer them. This corresponds with the apologetic hope that Ted Barnett has for the program:

> TEE plays a critical role in protecting the local church from the increasingly anti-Christian posture of Islam, local cults, and syncretistic religious groups. And it helps equip church leaders to address cultural issues that have historically challenged African Christian theology-issues like witchcraft, ancestor veneration, divination, and polygamy. (1991, 5)

Conclusion

CECA's administrator envisions evaluation as a means of "knowing what our students have learned, what must be taught again, and what must be added to our programme" (Way 1985, 9).

The evaluation of top level leaders was split three ways. One, a missionary, felt the program was fulfilling its aims. The national director was more cautious, replying that the program is "somewhat" fulfilling its aims. And the third said, "Yes and no!" Further discussion with these leaders revealed that the heaviest factor giving weight to the negative was finances.

Were the whole financial picture of the country better, this program would be a shining example of TEE as a nonformal type of leadership development.

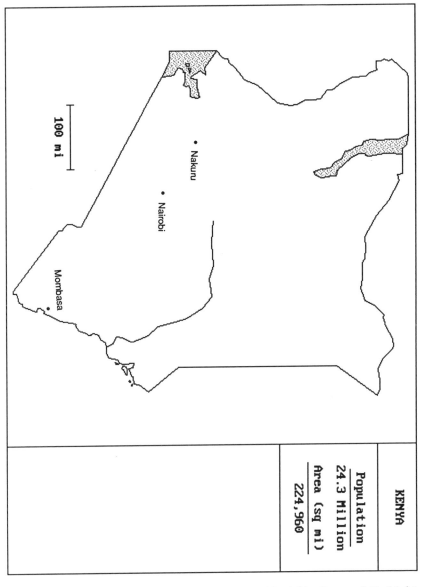

100 mi

• Nakuru

• Nairobi

Mombasa
•

KENYA

Population
24.3 Million

Area (sq mi)
224,960

CHAPTER SEVEN

From Nakuru to Nairobi

How could a TEE program go from 900 students down to only 100, and then back up to nearly 500 again? The problems which caused such a decline and the solutions which resolved them make up the story of one of the oldest TEE programs in Africa. It is set in the urban and rural areas widely scattered across Kenya where the Africa Inland Church (AIC) and the Africa Inland Mission (AIM) have planted churches, now organized under AIC into twenty-four districts.

In 1969 AIM missionaries Frew and Davis started talking of TEE. The church decided to begin a program in 1971-1972. Scott Theological College agreed to integrate TEE with the College (but this did not materialize). Dick Dunkerton became the first director of AIC-TEE in Nakuru in 1975, and in the following years taught key leaders in the church about TEE, helped start classes, and trained people for TEE. In just four years he developed AIC-TEE to its apex of 900 students. Dunkerton eventually left Kenya for service in Lesotho.

The program was decentralized in 1979, and each region managed its own affairs without a central office. A pervasive misunderstanding also began to grow between TEE and the church council regarding the purpose of the program. A decline set in, and by 1988 the program had reached its low point of 100 students.

In 1986 AIC, alarmed by the near collapse of their TEE program, asked AIM missionary Phillip Turley to help them redevelop the program. A committee was formed to study the problems leading to the decline. After two years they presented their recommendations.

The church was sorry that many Christians stopped studying the old TEE programme, so they formed a committee to study the problem. The committee found that there was much confusion about who should study TEE. There was also confusion about what kind of certificate a TEE student should get. Could a TEE student become a pastor when he finishes? The Committee thought about all the problems and then came up with two new programs. In the future, the church wants to develop an extension program for training pastors. But for now they saw that the TEE books were useful for training church members to know the Bible and learn how to serve God. (Turley 1990, 18)

The committee reported that the TEE program was capable of great positive impact on the church in Bible knowledge and service. However, the original aim of AIC-TEE, to train pastors, was not being fulfilled. A change in the purpose of the program, to the development and training of lay leaders, was recommended. To emphasize this shift in focus, a new name was chosen: Biblical Education by Extension (BEE). The committee also recommended that the central office be reconstructed. The resultant program was a centralized lay training program, and AIC-BEE was born. Turley was appointed BEE national coordinator in 1988. In four years the program grew from 100 to 500 students.

Aim of the Program

BEE is a Bible study program designed to train lay leadership for the church (Turley 1990, 18). When it was decided to retain the program on a basic level for general church training, Ephesians 4:12 was adopted as a motto: "Training God's people for works of service." That which started out *to train pastors* now became a tool *for pastors to use* in training the members of their congregation to serve the Lord.

As one BEE board member related, different kinds of church leaders, who help the pastor, are sharpened. A young pastor/tutor affirmed that "BEE will help our churches, because if a student knows the Word of God, he will spread that knowledge to many who don't." BEE gives substance to the verbal witness of Christians to their communities.

Larry Bardwell, a BEE regional coordinator, is thrilled by the possibilities he sees of using the program to develop key leaders in the church. His home church originally commissioned him to reach the unreached through discipleship. Now he can do this by fulfilling the aim of the BEE leadership model: to train the *laos,* enabling them in turn to reach out and train others.

Administration

A BEE national coordinator, selected by AIC, oversees the program in conjunction with a BEE board. Each region forms its own BEE committee and selects a regional coordinator. The chairmen of these committees and the regional coordinators (two men from each region) comprise the national BEE board. The regional coordinator liaisons with the national coordinator and class leaders. Classes are begun on a local level with permission from the church council.

Centralization

When the TEE program was decentralized in 1979, an immediate decline was noticed. There were only two or three regional coordinators in place at the time, and no structure by which a decentralized administration could be run. Each region carried on as best they could under the circumstances. The problems included lack of regional office space, no finances for administration, no uniformity of standards for grading and certificates, no central keeping of records and fees, class leaders not turning to a central office for help and training, little networking across regions or training in administration.

The BEE national coordinator has now pulled the reins of control back into a central office. The national office maintains all student records and keeps track of fees. A class record sheet is submitted, and certificates issued on the basis of those records. Classes cannot receive their certificates until their records and fees have come into the central office. All certificates are issued promptly from the national office and must be signed by the BEE national coordinator to be valid.

Class leaders are awarded certificates of merit for prompt and complete submission of fees and records to central office. When they have earned three certificates of merit, they are also given a lovely gold pin inscribed with the letters BEE above a red cross over which is superimposed an open Bible. These are presented each year at an awards ceremony for class leaders. This provides powerful motivation and reward for good administration. After the first awards ceremony, records and fees began to arrive at central office with great dispatch.

A central inventory of books was established and maintained. By buying the books in large quantities, the central office was able to get them at a lower price. During the decentralized phase, regional coordinators and class leaders often purchased books at retail prices from local book stores. The AEAM Text-Africa series is published in

Kenya. Therefore AIC-BEE escapes the higher costs of shipping and customs that other countries have to pay. Nevertheless, the difference between retail and wholesale prices represents a substantial savings. Savings are passed on in two ways. The program was able to offer the books to the students at a lower price; and one free book was provided for class leaders.

Nonformal Nature

AIC-BEE, nonformal in nature, has no links with any existing academic institution. Grades and certificates are given to students from the BEE program. No graduation ceremonies or special days of recognition are held at this time for students (one is held annually for tutors).

The program has expressed the desire that every Bible School make the BEE Teacher Training Course a two-or-three-hour credit within its curriculum (Turley 1989, 2). Since 1990, BEE graduates (those successfully completing 32 BEE courses) who meet the entrance requirements of Kapsabet Bible College will receive first year credit, entering as second year students into either the resident or extension programme of that school (Summary 1990, 3).

Finances

Turley firmly believes that if there is a strong administration, the financial base will be correspondingly strengthened; if administration weakens, the financial structure will reflect that. Administrative and financial strength directly correlate.

Students pay a fee, collected by the teacher and sent into the central office, and purchase their books through the teacher. AIM also contributes to AIC-BEE through the Key Workers Fund, out of which the salary of the national coordinator comes. Regional coordinators and class leaders receive no BEE salary; they are frequently pastors receiving a church stipend.

Financial reports for the two years immediately following the re-establishment of a centralized program (October 1, 1989 to September 30, 1990; and October 1, 1990 to March 1991) confirm the correlation between administrative and financial strength. They show for one thing a great increase in fees collected at the central office. When an administration is loosely run, records and fees are sometimes lost.

Centralization of book sales also reflects financial stability. "For the first time in the department's history, we are now earning more money from book sales than we are actually spending to buy them" (Turley 1991b, 2). This is "attributable to the policy change at the end of 1988 and the growth of the BEE program" (1).

Forming Classes

Classes are begun on a local level as the need is seen. When a BEE teacher wishes to form a new class, it is necessary to obtain permission from the church council. Whether formed from members of a local church or from members of a branch or district level, the appropriate body must give permission. When a student wishes to join a BEE class, he fills out a student application and has it signed by the chairman of his church council. The teacher then sends it to the national coordinator along with his class records, and the national coordinator opens a student file for him.

Regional Coordinators

Regional coordinators are appointed by regional church councils. Whether missionary or national, they work for and report directly to the regional church council. They attend regional BEE committee meetings and national BEE board meetings. They liaison with the national coordinator, and deal with the central office for administrative purposes, such as purchase of books and organization of new classes in their region.

Ideally, they should be a source of local promotion of BEE, encouragement and training for teachers, and reinforcement and assistance to the national coordinator. They ought to visit and talk with their teachers about the problems they are facing, to keep their hands on the pulse of the program.

Indeed, some regional coordinators fulfill this ideal. Besides teaching classes themselves, they have regular meetings with the teachers and provide in-service training on various issues, such as how to handle class questions, and development of group dynamics. Through the efforts of these coordinators, the program is immeasurably strengthened.

Some regional coordinators, very busy with their duties within the church, find such policies difficult to carry out. Even if they see the need and have the vision, their schedules are overburdened. At other times, a coordinator may be in the position of overseeing BEE teachers, while he himself has never taught a BEE class. This can form a stumbling block to enthusiastic development in that region.

Component Parts

Students

Students must be Christians in good fellowship with the church. This is ascertained by the local church council. "It is best if (the student) has finished up to Grade 5" (Turley 1990, 18). In early 1991 there were 496 active BEE students (Biannual Report 1991, 1).

Students range from good church members, men's and women's leaders, elders, Sunday School teachers, and youth leaders, on up to evangelists and lay pastors. For example, Isaac, a headmaster in a secondary school and an elder in his church, is for all practical purposes a pastor. He uses his BEE lessons for preaching material, for counseling problems, and for his own personal growth.

Students themselves emphasize that BEE is a form of training which motivates and enables them to share their faith more easily. I heard some exclaim that they wish every born-again Christian could study through BEE.

Self-study Material

TEE began its program in Kenya by using the AEAM Text-Africa series from Evangel Publishing House in Nairobi and continues to use these as a majority of its texts in BEE. The strength of this series lies in its impact on practical application to service. Students and class leaders alike testify that participants "have gone out to use what they are studying in class."

The programming method used in these texts also facilitates learning. One student explained the contents of the opening lessons of the book *Following Jesus* (Selfridge 1974) in a neat summary form to me.

Along with the AEAM-Text Africa series comes the philosophy usually predicated as "the book is your teacher." There are both positive and negative sides to this philosophy. A good reason to emphasize the book as your teacher is to stem teacher-lectures during class time. The teacher does not need to present a lecture repeating material already learned from the text. While that is good, such a philosophy is overdone if it reduces the significant human role of the leader. The book as the only teacher would be a negative.

The AEAM series has no books on pastoral training, homiletics, theology, or counseling. *The Shepherd and His Work* (Crider and Msweli, 1974) gives some basics but is limited in scope. This was a problem when TEE was seen as pastoral training but has less importance in a lay training scenario such as BEE.

When AEAM began its series, the goal was 40 books to comprise a basic Bible study curriculum. These books were made available one by one as they were written and published over the years. At this stage, 35 titles are off the presses; others are in various stages nearing publication. In practical terms, this means that the older programs wait with some anxiety for more titles to bring to their students.

Furthermore, no definite curriculum or standard for graduation had been set. In BEE, as in most schools, neither teachers nor students knew when a student had completed the program. To handle this problem, BEE established a defined curriculum with a definite terminus for its own use. Each student must take 32 courses: 20 of these are required, and the remaining 12 may be chosen from a list of electives. The majority are AEAM-Text Africa, but others include seminars, AIC material, and training under AIC's Christian Education Department. On completion of these requirements, a graduate receives a Certificate of Biblical Studies, signed by the Bishop of the AIC, the national BEE coordinator, and the chairman of the national BEE committee (Summary 1990, 3).

Service in the Church

Since students are Christians in good fellowship with the church, most serve the church throughout their BEE experience. Skills are developed in Bible study, prayer, witnessing, and leadership. Students lead services, visit the sick, and bring others into the church. Some who teach Sunday School speak of adapting and modifying the lessons to give children the benefit of the knowledge they have gained through BEE. And (although BEE is not strong on pastoral training) some teach and preach from the pulpit. Malinda, a layman in Nairobi, studied BEE courses for many years. He was then given the responsibility to pastor a church. He is one who functions as a pastor and teaches a BEE class as well. With God's blessing, there will continue to be many more stories like this.

Discussion Seminars

A class leader gave me a brief outline of his discussion seminar. "The students come and I welcome them; . . . after asking a few questions about (how) they are and what they are doing, we pray. After prayer we do the first part, (test) questions (in the book). We see what they studied at home, and start the discussion questions-those we really need to talk about with one another." He went on to explain that if students have difficulty with the lesson, they could ask for help, and this might lead into a discussion as well. As to the theory underlying discussion classes, I could not fault him.

Reportedly, good interaction takes place in many of the classes. One longtime student and class leader testified that while the class was supposed to take one-and-a-half hours, it would sometimes take more than two hours because of time spent in discussion. The discussion method of BEE is popular with the people. Some students testified that they like discussion, because it "increases my knowledge of truth." Interaction is more frequent between teacher and students, and to a lesser degree between student and student. One student commented on the fact that his leader did not let one person monopolize the discussion but made the classes interesting.

A question arises as to how much problem solving goes on in these discussions. A tendency to stick to the lesson prevails. One leader reported too much discussion of trivia. He felt that leaders needed to focus discussion on major issues-like the significance of the death of Christ—and move away from discussions on how many hours He spent in the tomb. Some students said problems *were* discussed in their class.

In an interview with one leader, I found that he has reserved a separate time for students to discuss pressing class problems: payment of books, unemployment and related problems impinging on payment of fees, and personal problems. Many do not perceive BEE as a means of problem-solving, because it has not been stressed as a main purpose of discussion.

Teacher/Tutor

In BEE the paradigm of TEE has shifted to the teacher. Instead of three components: the book, the class, and in-service training (as illustrated in the fence model), Turley uses the illustration of a three-legged stool. The first leg represents the book, the second leg the weekly class meeting, the third leg ministry practice. These three connect to the most important, the seat, which represents the teacher. The legs are inserted into the seat and completed by it. When you have the seat into which the legs fit, you have a useful stool. Without the seat, the legs become firewood.

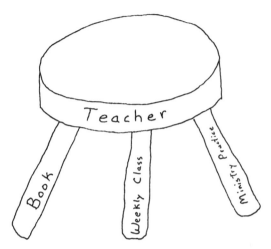

Figure 4. Stool Analogy

The reason Turley has come to this model is that without the teacher, you have neither BEE nor TEE. If teachers are not faithful in all their duties, students will get discouraged and quit. If they lecture and are boring, students will get discouraged and quit. Teachers not only have to provide an interesting class-above all else they must model the truths being taught. The program will only be as strong as those who teach. "Without strong, skillful teachers, the new BEE programme cannot succeed. It is time that we ... begin to invest more into our teachers, the heart of the program" (Turley, 1989, 1).

This philosophy is embodied in Proverbs 27:17, "As iron sharpens iron, so a man sharpens another." A book makes a helpful tool in the teaching process, but the most important component is the one who models the principles being taught, the human component. The book communicates a lot of information, but we need to see that information modelled as a life style and as skills for ministry.

In the class I observed, I felt that English was used to please me, whereas normally they use Swahili (and English). I sensed that my presence flustered the leader. However, that leader displayed an enthusiasm that was and is the biggest factor in the continuance and growth of his class. A motivated teacher truly motivates his students. He would have profited even more from some coaching on the dynamics of group discussion.

Teacher Training

The present method being implemented by Turley for new teachers involves them in a BEE Teacher Training Course, covering BEE principles and policy in about 25 hours of teaching time. The new class leader then teaches his first course under supervision by either the Regional Coordinator or another BEE teacher. Developing skills in group dynamics denote that the teacher is under training during this period.

All teachers need to hone the skills of group discussion. The ability to lead a discussion class does not come naturally to many people. Like learning to ride a bicycle, it comes with practice under tutelage. This type of experience can develop not only teaching skills, but confidence as well (Turley 1989, 2). The supervisor can meet privately with the new teacher to give input and gain feedback. This period closes with a debriefing session after the teacher has completed his first book.

Turley envisions further upgrading of the Teacher Training Course. He would rather see controlled growth with quality teachers well trained, than see the program mushrooming in size only. Discussion leaders' guides are in preparation. A special paper entitled "Leading Good Discussion" has been prepared for use with all prospective teachers.

Pastors are busy people, some with as many as seven churches to look after. It is no wonder that a training class in extension methods might be considered a burden to their overfull responsibilities. Yet an increasing number are asking for in-service training. If the increasing interest can be followed up, tremendous growth within the program should result in the years ahead. This pattern also highlights the importance of pastors. If pastors have no vision for a program, it will be difficult to implement. If pastors feel the need, it is time to respond.

In Kenya, distance is always a factor. New teachers out in remote areas on their own don't have the opportunity of being trained or supervised. Turley feels that bringing them in to a central locality and training them before they begin classes is more fruitful.

Some Bible Schools are giving students training in BEE methods. I visited a young pastor who was trained for BEE in Bible School and encouraged to go out and begin classes.

AIC-BEE presently has 80 centers in operation with 45 teachers. Additional class leaders need to be trained. With the present vision of the BEE program, five training sessions were conducted during the first six months of 1991. BEE will thrive on sound well-trained class leaders.

Spiritual Foundation

The spiritual formation of the *laos* remains the foundation of the AIC-BEE program. An article written for "Today in Africa" encourages church members to study through BEE for spiritual growth:

> Discovering the truth about our sin is painful. However, once we confess our sin and continue reading the Bible, it is like finding the hidden honeycomb. God's Word becomes sweet as we discover His love for us, His promises to us, and His provision for us. (Turley 1990, 18)

External Relationships

Several problems plague the BEE program in Kenya, and many of them are in some way related to a very important external factor: the relationship between BEE and the church.

One such problem surfaced in the budget. Not enough money in the budget prevents allocating necessary funds to the BEE program. The church leaders do not consider it a high-enough priority.

The geography and vast distances of Kenya present a related factor. A large number of pastors, many of them scattered in remote rural areas, never had the chance to go through a BEE training program during their time in Bible School. To reeducate them would take time, expense, and travel to distant places. It becomes difficult to involve them in and derive their support for a program with which they are not thoroughly acquainted.

Conversely, shortage of funds prevents traveling to needy areas and conducting seminars, which in part advertise the program. It takes money to make the value of the program known; and unless the value of the program becomes known you cannot expect support. Says one pastor, the "oblivion" of the program prevents the necessary support being given.

The problem of acceptance is reflected in missionary departures from BEE work. Once a missionary begins to work, he may find that regional and national leaders not only ignore BEE, but even criticize it. This cuts motivation to continue. In cases where church leaders don't particularly want the program, missionaries become discouraged (Report 1991, 1).

The original TEE program ran into trouble because it was outside the experience of the church that *nonformal* education could produce qualified leaders. Pastors conditioned to a European educational pattern did not accept as adequate anything outside of the formal resident Bible Schools through which they were trained. After all, the church had been established in 1895 and had trained its pastors in resident Bible Schools from the start. Resistance to TEE training was based on this outlook.

And now, on the verge of turning the BEE program over to a Kenyan coordinator, the leaders of the church still balk. There is an elusive feel to the approval of money and personnel for BEE. The transition brings out troubled feelings to the effect that missionaries begin things, then leave and turn them over to nationals, expecting that the church will help with funds. The church doesn't think it has the resources.

The new BEE program has in fact made great strides toward financial self-sufficiency. And the mission has not left the church holding the financial bag. Yet a more wholehearted church acceptance and approval is needed.

I believe the relationship with the national church constitutes the most crucial factor in the future success or failure of the BEE program.

Problems

Seven problems are listed here:

1. Movement of pastors within the denomination
2. Self-discipline and time
3. Lack of finances
4. Rapid expansion
5. Qualifications of tutors
6. Complexity of the model
7. Transitions in leadership

The background of some of these has already been explored.

Movement of Pastors

How the AIC assigns pastors constitutes a problem for the ongoing of BEE. The District Council assigns pastors and frequently changes those assignments on an annual basis. A pastor is seldom in one church for more than two or three years. If a pastor teaches a BEE class, he rarely has time to get a class well started before he is transferred out. The new pastor coming in may have no interest in BEE, and the class may die. The pastor who is transferred out often has to start a BEE class all over again in the new location. After years of such effort, he gets frustrated. Continuous transfer works against stable BEE classes.

Self-Discipline and Time

Home study demands great self-discipline. To sit down and study on a regular basis in a home situation is difficult. We honor the thousands who do this successfully. But it is a problem which each student must face and conquer. Great self-discipline is a prerequisite of extension.

Time constitutes another critical factor. As one leader expressed it: "the problem here is that the students work very late hours, and so we meet at night. We have seen the Lord work in our lives as we have (time) to study." Time and self-discipline are closely interlinked problems challenging BEE students.

Lack of Finances

Running a strong extension program demands major investment in teacher training, books, travel expenses, and administration. It requires money to make a good program go. Often rural people find it difficult financially to purchase books. The resources of Africa appear to be too meager to buy books and pay leaders. Some countries like Mozambique and Ethiopia can't obtain paper so the future of anything literary is clouded. Limited resources prevent greater progress.

Rapid Expansion

Rapid expansion will often kill a program. Problems have to be dealt with to accommodate swift growth. There must be an adequate teacher training program to supply qualified tutors, adequate equipment (books), and sufficient administrative structure. When a program mushrooms, even doctrinal soundness may be sacrificed if tutors untrained in biblical knowledge are pressed into service. Extension faces the mixed blessing of rapid expansion.

Unqualified Tutors

AIC-BEE uses any elder or pastor as class leader, regardless of his training. The need for training of BEE teachers is stressed against this background. Qualifications of a group leader are listed in every basic extension seminar. But with rapid expansion (see above), so much pressure is felt that any willing person is recruited.

Complexity of the TEE Model

TEE is a complex model, with an intricate balance of many parts, both internal and external. These are defined and discussed in the early chapters of this book. Getting the right kind of teachers lined up with the right kind of students, getting the right kind of ministry practice so students maximize their potential, getting the right kind of self-study material contextually written—all entails a program far more complex than at first meets the eye. It is more than listing and checking off the seven component parts and the four external relationships. To construct a TEE program demands a kind of analysis and attention to detail which must be taught to others if they are to take over its leadership.

Transitional Issues

When missionary or national directors turn over a TEE program to other national leaders, the program enters a transitional period. If the incoming leader is not versed in the analytical skills necessary to do the job, difficulties will follow. If the reins of the program are turned over to a missionary or national who doesn't have the vision for or real interest in the progress of the program but takes that leadership only because it has been assigned to him, the program will be undermined.

Sometimes the selection process used within the secular nation affects the selection process of leaders for ministry projects within the church. Nationally speaking, there are only so many openings for university graduates. Preferences are often ignored and persons who have skills in one area are arbitrarily put into another line of work.

People in Kenyan secular society do not have as many options as Americans, nor as much freedom of choice in what they will undertake as a vocation. A person trained in the arts may be given a job in science, because there *are* no available openings in the field of art. This carries over into the church and BEE, where the selection process may bring forth inappropriate leaders. Interest, desire, training, giftedness, and capability are not always the primary considerations, as they ought to be. Sometimes people gifted in one area are placed arbitrarily to fulfill a need in another area. This happens in the missionary shuffle, as furloughs come and go. It happens in our culture in America in the great Peter Principle.

In transition now, BEE needs to continue to develop under new, national leadership. The new leader, Mr. Manyasia, appointed in 1986, deferred his leadership till he completed his training at Scott Theological College. He is taking over from Turley now.

Transition times can be difficult. The administrative challenge is great. The financial challenge likewise. He has the provision of a house and a small salary. BEE student fees cover only postage and a few of the office expenses. Manyasia feels the weight of winning further church approval. He cites lack of acceptance by some missionary and church leaders as a hindrance, and feels that unless wholehearted support for the program is generated, serious consequences may result.

Innovations

AIC-BEE has a new and innovative emphasis on the teacher and teacher training. They have provided curriculum guidelines for graduation standards and introduced a number of new courses for credit. A refreshing attempt to teach a wider range of subjects and skills, and the introduction of variety in course presentation, comprise attempts at innovation.

Evaluation

John Mutevu, chairman of the BEE board, maintains that BEE progress is encouraging. Many people are being trained according to the level of their education. Another board member points out that the statistics of growth over the last four years, and the good BEE has done the church, promise a "very bright future."

The program is running at a reasonably low cost, yet it is highly dependent on sources of revenue outside the extension students themselves. African economies are in a decline, and the ability to pay for BEE courses will decline also. Economic realities present a very severe test of extension programs.

The need for evaluation of the program by church leaders is essential. They must compare the blessings of the program with the cost of the program. Using preferred criteria, the African Inland Church will determine the future of BEE in Kenya. In the meantime, much work will be required to create a favorable climate for BEE in the church as a whole.

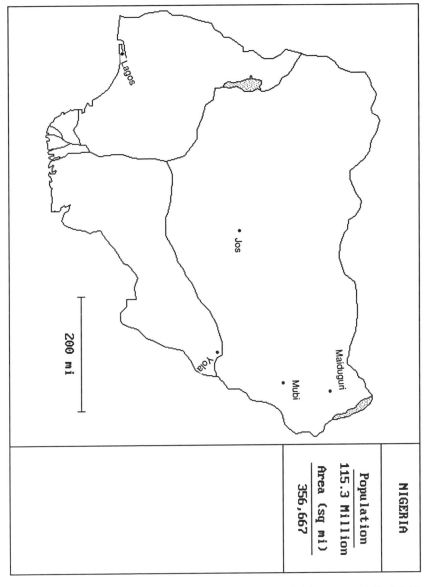

NIGERIA

Population
115.3 Million
Area (sq mi)
356,667

200 mi

Lagos

Jos

Yola

Mubi

Maiduguri

CHAPTER EIGHT

From Jos to Maiduguri and Back

We covered nearly 900 miles as we travelled from Jos to Maiduguri, Numan to Nyola, and back to Jos. On the highways in that northeast corner of Nigeria, children filled big potholes in the tarmac roads with dirt. They held out their hands in hope that grateful motorists would throw them a little money in return for their work. Some of those potholes were big, but the new stretches of super highway also reflect the fact that Nigeria is one of the most progressive countries on the continent.

TEE fills the many gaps in local church leadership in Nigeria. I was able to interview many leaders and TEE students there, imbibing their hopes, fears, and problems as they lead the largest extension program in Africa.

Aim of the Program

The Accrediting Council for Theological Education in Africa (ACTEA) has ranked the Church of Christ in Nigeria Extension Bible School (COCIN-EBS) as the largest single TEE program in Africa. The program was begun in 1972 with one hundred students. In 1990, COCIN had 3800 students and 300 tutors.

The original aim was to give more Bible training to evangelists who only had one year of residential Bible school. The evangelists of COCIN often found themselves taking care of churches they had planted, functioning much as pastors. Their in-service training was to prepare them for a pastoral function.

But shortly that aim was broadened. "Later on, the courses were opened to all communicant members, with the aim of helping them to grow spiritually and to equip them for the Lord's work, (that all might) serve Him effectively and faithfully" (Brief History 1990, 1).

This aim fulfilled a deep felt need. COCIN started their EBS program for evangelists and broadened it because they lacked manpower to meet the leadership needs of the church. Davou Giyang, Director of COCIN-EBS, emphasized to me that the program is open to everyone, not only evangelists, but all catechists.

Dan Pochi, former Director of COCIN-EBS, points out that the original aim of further training for evangelists was fulfilled in those early days and is still being fulfilled. But with the success of the program came the desire to include the whole church. Every person needs to study the Word of God. The leaders hope that church members will grow in ability to serve as they study, and that some may go on to become evangelists and fulltime workers.

Now COCIN-EBS, viewed as part of the Christian Education arm of the Church of Christ, gives general Bible training for all the church members with an emphasis on leadership. But whether on the Extension Bible School level or the advanced level, ordination is not a blanket aim. Many lay leaders are being developed. The program is fulfilling its aims, because "it is producing a lot of manpower in the churches today" (Pochi 1990a).

Administration

The head of the program is called the director or principal. He is responsible to the church for the effective administration of the program. He is assisted by regional supervisors, who at one time were paid staff but now are not.

A great network of regions and districts spans the northeast corner of Nigeria. The COCIN principal usually spends a week each year in each of these areas, coaching and helping supervisors and class leaders. The length and breadth of the work is astounding. Supervisors obtain their books and texts from the central office in Jos, many miles away. Communication is not easy. Just the mechanics of selection and delivery of courses and related papers for each new term boggles the mind. Occasional mix-ups occur over certificates and tests, but these do not significantly hinder the progress of EBS.

The program is divided into two distinct parts: a basic Bible school and an advanced program. The advanced course is called Extension Theological College (ETC) and has its own coordinator for administrative purposes.

The basic Extension Bible School consists of three sections. The first, called Basic Course 1 (B1), is a module of six AEAM Text-Africa courses—one a term, for two years. The second or Basic Course 2 (B2), consists of a further module of six courses—one a term, for two years. It takes a minimum of four years to finish the basic courses.

A Post District Bible School of two additional years is held on a certificate level. It is offered to those who have completed residential Bible School or those who have finished B1 and B2 courses. Not all who start TEE in B1 choose to continue studies in the Post District Bible School.

The advanced program, begun in 1990, offers a Diploma in Theology and takes four to six years to complete. The course is open to those who are high school graduates and have sufficient background in English. It equips them spiritually and academically to serve the Lord. The church may ordain graduates as clergymen (Brief History 1990, 2).

Working Organization

1. The director is the chief executive officer. He visits as many classes as possible each year. Pochi, for instance, often travelled 15,000 kilometers (7,500 miles) a year out to the districts as principal. He found that where EBS is functioning well, an annual visit is sufficient. But in areas where the program is weak, it demands more attention, and the principal may visit there two or three times a year.

2. Regional supervisors oversee TEE activity in their area, lessening the work load of the principal. District supervisors are responsible to work under a regional supervisor. They train teachers in the region by holding sample classes throughout each module. A district supervisor may have as many as sixteen teachers from the basic B1, B2, and Post District Bible School under his care, with whom he meets regularly.

3. Editors are responsible for production of new books and validation of translations of AEAM texts as they become available. They also compose test papers for the classes.

4. The bursar maintains financial transactions and keeps centralized records. He meets with supervisors to gather fees and is responsible to the director.

5. The typist types all correspondence and is responsible for preparing books for printing.

6. The storekeeper maintains a stock of books in a warehouse. COCIN maintains this supply for all programs associated with the Theological Education by Extension Association of Nigeria (TEEAN). The key is to prepare for the long haul by having enough materials for all as required. Subsidy is needed to lay in enough books (Pochi 1990b, 95-97).

Duties of the Director

1. The director oversees the distribution of books within COCIN-EBS. This includes taking manuscripts of books, written by COCIN for use in their program, to the printer. He also receives requests for books and arranges for their transport to the regional supervisors. Regional supervisors take them to the district supervisors, who distribute them to teachers for their classes.

2. The director visits supervisors and teachers in the various regions. Some regional supervisors, lacking means of transport, will travel with the director on his visits to see the district supervisors and tutors. The director may come without notice and therefore gets an accurate picture of how the program is progressing. As Pochi said, it takes a lot of "running up and down!"

3. The director keeps all the student records in files in his office. Regional supervisors come in and check those records to make sure they are accurate. There is a report card for every course. A colorful certificate is awarded to students when they have completed both B1 and B2, and a second certificate is given for the completion of Post District Bible school. The teacher has the student fill out a form when he is eligible for a certificate. This is passed on up to the regional supervisor for signature, then on to the director who is responsible to cross-check class registers and make sure the student's course work is complete before awarding the certificate.

4. The director has oversight of the central office and finances, and the work of the typist and bursar.

Extension Bible School has a system involving three standard receipts for financial transactions. The teacher collects fees from the students and gives a receipt. He gives the money to the regional supervisor and receives a receipt from him. The supervisor turns the money over to the director who also gives a receipt for funds received.

An accurate record of books is also kept. Upon delivery of books to regional supervisors, a voucher is signed. Supervisors must return either the money or the books after each course.

5. The fifth duty is trouble-shooting. When people indicate that they have problems, the principal sets a time and place where they can gather and begins a round table of counselling. He tries to find out why the problem has developed and tries to get them on target again. If it applies (such as situations where students and church people have misconceptions about TEE), he explains the design of the program. He has found that understanding will precede a renewal of the program. These visits are important because people say, "Ah, now we know that we are in a school, now that we see our principal."

Regional Supervisors

In Africa, intermediary cadres who link the central office with outlying tutors are in vogue. COCIN Extension calls them supervisors. Sometimes other terms—overseer, regional coordinator or zonal leader—are used. They are appointed full-time or part-time to oversee EBS activities in a specific geographic region. They usually come up through the system—student, tutor, district supervisor, and finally regional supervisor. Their duties include:

1. Visiting each EBS class in their area once a term.

2. Training tutors to lead classes.

3. Assessing class performance of students and tutors. Particular note is taken of the discussion session. An assessment form is prepared in duplicate for the teacher and the supervisor, to check improvement on the next visit.

4. Marking tests and giving grades.

5. Collecting books from the central store and distributing them to teachers, who in turn give them to students at the beginning of each term.

6. Collecting fees from teachers and sending them to the central office.

A retreat is held periodically, Pochi told me, to train supervisors in record keeping, how to collect money and remit it to headquarters, supervision of materials, the discussion method, and how to lead demonstration classes at the weekly tutor's meeting.

The job of regional supervisor is both intricate and difficult. Y. B. Malafa is regional supervisor for the whole of Borno State and has six district supervisors under him, and 107 teachers—40 teachers in one district, 30 in another, 11 in Goza district, 15 in Bala, and 11 in Nguru. Borno District alone has 700 Extension Bible School students and 40 advanced level students.

The regional supervisor works with his district supervisors to train teachers. Commonly, they hold a sample class each week for the tutors, displaying methods that can be used with that lesson, answering questions, and training tutors in discussion methods. These training classes are divided into those who do their classes in English and those who teach in the vernacular.

Rev. Daniel Gula, a regional supervisor, and his wife Miriam, not only train tutors but lead EBS classes as well. They have more experienced district supervisors who hold teacher training classes in places where they are unable to visit due to time and distance. TEE is about people, people involved with each other, people close together. Relationships develop naturally out of these productive sessions.

The regional supervisors mark all tests, give grades to students, and keep grade records. Tests are held once every two weeks, with a final test after ten weeks. Supervisors compile all these grades and send them to the central office in Jos for certification. This viable administrative pattern works because of real commitment on the part of the leaders, proper division of labor, and creativity in handling problems.

Most supervisors are part-time. They are often pastors and do not have much time. In dividing attention between EBS and church, they struggle to do a thorough job. To alleviate this pressure, COCIN is trying to revive the office of regional supervisor as a paid position so that more can assume it on a full-time basis and afford travel. The more travel a regional supervisor can do, the more help he is to the director. Distance and the necessity of delegation of duties make the position of regional supervisor crucial. Pochi says, "Good supervision on a regular basis keeps a TEE program going...a poorly supervised program collapses" (1990b, 102).

Central Office and Storeroom

Besides a spacious office for the director, bursar, and typist, COCIN also has a large storeroom for books. When I walked into the storeroom, my feeling was that this is the way TEE should be operated. Books are ordered well in advance of classes. Large metal boxes are stacked near the door, ready for use when books are distributed to regional supervisors. Supervisors are far away and have little room to store books and test papers. COCIN-EBS purchased the boxes so that storage problems in the regions would be avoided, an excellent innovation for a hot and dusty land where paper materials may easily be destroyed.

Component Parts

Type of Student

Not only do laypeople without any previous training become students in COCIN's program, but pastors and other Bible school graduates take EBS courses. One student reports that he has received instruction from the TEE material which he never had while studying in Bible school before he became a pastor. He testifies that all the pastors he knows have kept on studying in EBS.

Most local church leaders also take TEE. I talked to the wife of an EBS student who began to study about a year and a half ago. She was pleased with her husband's efforts: he was managing his family, studying in EBS, sometimes preaching in the church, and liking his studies very much.

Most students go on to complete B1 and B2 and remain active in the church. "It is hoped," the director said, "that after completion people who feel that God is leading them to full-time ministry may be ordained by the church. However (the student) doesn't have to be ordained. It does not mean he will not work for the Lord. He will actually be a preacher wherever he is" (Pochi 1990a). And that is what is happening in this program.

Self -Study Material

COCIN uses the AEAM Text-Africa programmed books. They have written four of their own programmed books as well for use in the Post District Bible School. These are also used by other extension schools which are a part of TEEAN (TEE Association of Nigeria).

Emphasis is placed on completing the book, and tutors and students are well acquainted with the philosophy "the book is the teacher." One man said, "The book itself is the lecturer!"—an apt remark, since he took his lecture from the book and his discussion and application from the guidance of the tutor. No excuse is accepted for not finishing the book. If some are hindered because of the press of work and family problems, they are not given a passing grade. However, if they finish the book and do well in class work, this is seen as a mitigating factor and taken into account if their exam grade is low.

More than one expressed the wish that the EBS books could be translated into other Nigerian languages besides Hausa, such as the Kanuri language used by many Muslims in northeast Nigeria.

The higher level courses use a series from England (and in the English language). Students say the new material is harder because there is a great deal of reading before the questions at the end of the chapter, and the questions do not coordinate well with the lesson material. Others wish that in the higher level there would be more contextualization as is done in the Text Africa series. One very intelligent business lady made the comment that the higher level books ought to be programmed in small-step learning. Even higher level material needs to be organized into blocks of easy learning for efficient study by busy laypeople.

Service in the Church

Pochi emphatically states that the church has already seen the benefit of TEE, "because while (students) study, they give part-time service to the church. The church is the initial practicing ground for what they learn" (1990b, 12).

As one supervisor expressed it, participants go and preach or go and discuss with somebody about Christ, and then they relate this in class. "It's mandatory for that student to go. When he goes, he is expected to have a market (for the gospel)... this encourages them and they put these (lessons) into practice." He rated all students highly on this type of assignment.

Discussion Seminars

The most intimate part of TEE, one leader told me, is the discussion group. Finishing the books can be mechanical, but the heartbeat of TEE is the discussion. Students are encouraged to bring their opinions out into the light and to test them against the group and against the Word of God. Openness and willingness to share are developed.

Madi, a tutor, reported that in his class, discussion crosses in all directions. Students talk to one another as well as to him. Mala Simon, another tutor, said that in his group, discussion was inclusive. Almost everybody expressed themselves. Another group leader told how he gets the discussion going so easily that students interact with one another without further overt reference to him. Only when something difficult arises which needs explanation and input does he interject. High interest is sustained and students often carry on discussion, urging the tutor to let them continue past closing time.

Learning takes place through this interchange of ideas. Tutors and students learn from each other. One tutor said that even though he was a leader, he learned from those who were older and had more experience than he.

It was unequivocally agreed that the purpose of EBS discussion class is to deepen their relationship with Jesus Christ. Many testified of great changes that occurred in their lives through the discussion.

One of the first results, mentioned by both students and tutors, is spiritual growth. Growth occurs as Scripture is read and applied, lessons done, and key issues reflected on in class. Many of the burning issues of life are related to the lesson through discussion.

As an example, one believer testified that through the discussion class he had come to the conclusion that when a Christian is ill, it is better to lie down on his bed and hand over everything to the Lord than to become bitter and get medicine from the witchdoctor.

Some of the issues which are discussed in EBS class are spiritual life, marriage, family life, how to bring their children to Christ, suffering, spiritual and physical sickness, backsliding, life after death, the coming of Christ, and the resurrection body. Other issues like corruption in society, the education gap between young and old pastors, divorce, and a government ban on street preaching have also been discussed.

Higher level TEE (just began in 1990) has not had time to train tutors in discussion methods. Students therefore complain, saying leaders take too much time lecturing. They want to discuss the lesson and the issues of life.

The tutor is at the heart of discussion. He needs to understand and be trained in discussion methods. It is he who gets the discussion started with pertinent questions. When misunderstandings arise, he needs to know how to clarify, and when to hold back and let students clarify it between themselves. When disagreement arises, the tutor needs to direct the class in searching the Scripture to correct it.

Iliyasu, a regional supervisor, commented that if the class leader asks "yes" or "no" questions, discussion will not be easily started or sustained. He devised a way of asking questions so that "when the student opens his mouth, he has to say some sentences before closing it." I found this an ingenious way of describing the "how" and "why" questions so much needed. Questions from the programmed texts are often used by the tutors. Beyond that they must rely on their own reading and thinking to come up with discussion questions.

Teachers/Tutors

The tutors are volunteer class leaders responsible to the district and regional supervisor. They are part-time and do not receive a stipend, but the local church is responsible to help with their transport where necessary. They are chosen for their commitment to teaching the Word of God with knowledge. They must have a faithful character and be free of bad habits and moral problems. They must have passed B1 as the lowest educational requirement, though many have more than that, and some are even pastors with degrees. Their primary duties are:

1. Lead the weekly EBS discussion class.

2. Attend the teachers' meeting, a model of the discussion class held to prepare tutors to lead their own classes.

3. Keep records of each student: attendance, fees, assignments done, and exam grades.

4. Collect fees and pass them on to the supervisor.

Tutor Training

For tutors of the basic level Extension Bible School (B1, B2, and Post District Bible School), COCIN provides a workshop course which is conducted every two years. At that time new teachers are inducted. When a new group of teachers is beginning, it is important to have this general training.

In addition, a weekly teachers' meeting is held in which a sample class is done by the regional or district supervisors, to give tutors in-service training, with an emphasis on discussion methods.

Tutors are grateful for all the training they can get. The subjects in the texts are broad, and they encounter difficulties related to lack of knowledge and problems demanding skill and practice in discussion methods. COCIN publishes a teacher's guide to help them, giving step by step procedures for each class. One higher level leader who had not had any training (advanced level ETC was only begun in 1990 and training programs for that level were not yet established) was reteaching every line in the lesson instead of using the lesson for discussion.

Spiritual Foundation

The aims of the program, which were stated earlier, comprise the heart of the spiritual foundation of COCIN's extension school. EBS gets people into the Word, thus bringing them closer to their Savior. Many drastic changes for the better have occurred through study of the Word.

One tutor related a story reflective of the spiritual values of EBS. When a student is absent from class, he goes to visit him and find out the reason. Sometimes the reason hinges upon the fact that the student has gone to the spirits for help and is under conviction. Sometimes such a student will never return, but sometimes they can be brought to repentance, deeper understanding, and conviction, and return to class. A spiritual foundation is in place.

External Relationships

While the EBS program is closely tied to the COCIN denomination, church leadership must still be carefully cultivated.

Administrators of the church express general good feeling toward TEE. About 15 years ago, when the church was new to its EBS program, they backed it enthusiastically, giving high priority to funding and staffing. Missionary and national personnel built up TEE in a partnership. Recently, however, the church removed an experienced director under whom EBS had flourished (putting him into a higher church office outside of TEE) and replaced him with a man who was inexperienced and uninvolved in TEE.

In addition, they removed a valued translator and did not replace her at all, perhaps for funding reasons. If they highly valued the EBS program, would they not have given higher priority to the EBS staffing budget?

Pochi indicates that the church has seen the benefits of TEE (1990b, 120). Nevertheless he claims that there is an element within the church which centers solely on resident Bible School training. "Administrators of TEE, therefore, have a tough time trying to enlighten them on the viability of TEE as a good training method" (1990, 101). Pochi feels that any slackening of enthusiasm for the program would be disastrous because it would interrupt the development of leaders, the majority of whom take TEE.

Problems

Four problems head the list for COCIN-EBS: transport, transfers, finances, and transition periods.

Transport

Northeast Nigeria has vast distances, from Jos to Maiduguri to Numan and Nyola near the Cameroon border. These great distances are a problem to the program. They have spawned the creation of the post of supervisor. Now aid is needed to transport these supervisors. Public transport is not reliable. While the main roads are tarred, the back roads are rough. I saw several buses broken down on the side of the road as I traveled about. If TEE is to be conducted properly, adequate transport—a motorbike or car—is needed.

Transfers

Transfers by the government sometimes hinder the progress of students in completing their courses. People are moved to new areas and a tutor may lose a whole class. Now the program has a system whereby the students take a record card wherever they go. In this way they can continue to study without interruption.

One man had received three certificates for individual courses. When he was suddenly transferred he thought he had lost the opportunity to continue. But since he was transferred into Daniel Gula's area, he was able to keep on studying under COCIN without losing credit.

Lack of Funding

Financial aspects of EBS present COCIN with its biggest challenge. Money is needed for buying an adequate stock of books and for printing the Hausa translations. Without enough money for printing, some classes have to be delayed. Sometimes supervisors use their own money to buy books in advance of class to be sure to have them on hand. If there is a delay in collecting the fees, they suffer for that.

Students sometimes complain about fees (even though the church keeps costs as low as possible by subsidizing the price of books). One supervisor explained this complaint as the devil's attempt to discourage students by saying the fees are too much. He also pointed out that the church may give financial aid to students going to residential Bible schools, but is not accustomed to assisting TEE students.

TEE also needs money for supervisors' travel so that the program can succeed. The director receives a salary which helps him with travel. Local churches assist tutors with such local transport as is needed. But supervisors, whose job entails considerable travel, receive no assistance. Pochi experienced the result of funds drying up in the EBS program when the church said there were none available for regional supervisors. As director he then had to do much travel alone.

"In most cases the inability of the churches to support TEE is a result of the Nigerian economic recession which has adversely affected the financial buoyancy of the church within the last four years" (1990b, 100). In desperation the program has set its eyes on overseas grant organizations for financial support.

Transitions

The COCIN denomination transfers pastors periodically causing problems in EBS leadership. When the former director of EBS was sent to a pastorate, it meant a change in leadership for TEE.

When leadership is transferred in extension programs, careful scrutiny must be made of the qualifications and experience of the new leader. The choice of a leader lacking experience in TEE may well result in the program's crumbling. COCIN's program has still not entirely stabilized as a result of the last change. In times of transition, extension undergoes severe testing.

Innovations

The work of an additional intermediary person, the district supervisor, is crucial because the program is spread out over hundreds of miles in northeast Nigeria. The role of district supervisor keeps the program integrated. Such an innovation born out of necessity may well be the key to the program's future.

The beginning of a higher level TEE program in 1990, Extension Theological College (ETC), represents an important innovation because COCIN sees the many high school and college graduates who are active in the church as a source of local church ministry. I predict more extension programs in Africa will see this potential.

The church was very anxious to begin this program and continues to look for such students among their ranks who are able to cope with ETC work. ETC is giving western Nigeria for the first time a higher level program which grants a diploma in theology. The program includes students from other denominations and groups, such as Anglican, Lutheran, Brethren in Christ, and Baptist.

Evaluation

Obviously COCIN's TEE program has "done a lot of things for (our) country"—Nigeria. It has helped the church by training its leaders and given its people programs of Bible learning and active evangelism. The question the church must answer is whether or not it will rise to the challenge of providing the necessary effort and money to uphold and expand the program. The church must decide if, in view of the *following testimonies*, the spiritual blessings reported by tutors and students are worth the investment of personnel and money for this, the largest extension program in Africa.

"*Coming to TEE, I compared myself with the Bible. Now I am at home with my wife, with my kids around, and we chat and discuss the Bible.*"

"*When we came to the New Testament section, there was revealed some power within me...It was then I began to take part in church activities. I stopped drinking alcohol. Now at Nguru I am secretary for the church.*"

"*TEE helps a person witness wholeheartedly for Christianity...you can witness to anybody at anytime, being sure that because you have studied the Word you have something to deliver.*"

"*We have twenty who went to Bible colleges through studying TEE.*"

"*Through TEE a lot of them are greatly encouraged, so much so that they have volunteered to be evangelists.*"

"*Many families have been blessed in the sense that a lot of them have testified that their homes are no longer as they used to be, after studying this book*" (Christian Family Living, Conn and Simbiri 1978).

"*TEE has been very meaningful to me and very helpful to me. I was one of the first students that started the TEE program in 1972. ...I don't think anything would stop me from continuing TEE.*"

"*TEE directly helps me study the Bible every day.*"

"*In preaching, a TEE student uses some of the material that he studied in TEE. Anytime he preaches, comments come from the people, 'Oh, that's a great preacher'.*"

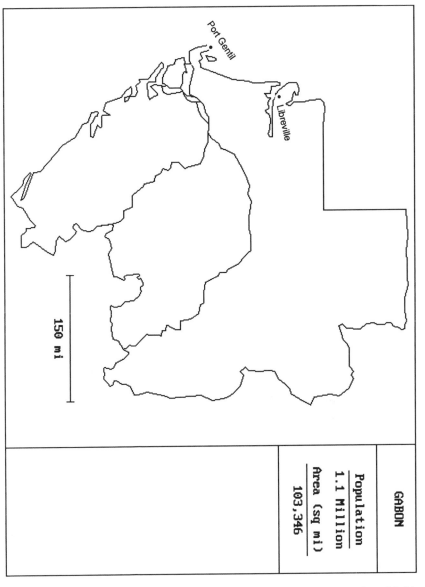

Port Genil

Libreville

150 mi

GABON

Population
1.1 Million

Area (sq mi)
103,346

Chapter Nine

From Libreville to Port Gentil

The night was warm and humid—the season of monsoon rains—and the area around the church was flooded two-feet deep in places. Loose planks across a steel frame formed a bridge—slippery, dark, narrow, with a handrail on one side. But inside the church a joyous welcome awaited us. This was the TEE class in Port Gentil, Gabon. Lively discussion and interest in the Word of God occupied the students' attention.

In 1946 the Christian and Missionary Alliance in Gabon founded a Bible School for pastoral training. This school ceased functioning in 1972.

In 1979 the national church agreed to try TEE as a training school for lay leaders. By 1980 it was operational, called in French the "Enseignement Theologique Decentralise (ETD) au Gabon." The TEE program of the C&MA in Gabon is only ten years old.

ETD (TEE) is set up on two levels. The Discipleship Level consists of 15 courses, open to all laypeople. The Servant Level is a continuation of the Discipleship Level, offering 15 advanced courses for those exercising a ministry in the church. Both levels run roughly parallel to the Ecole Biblique Bethel (a post-primary residence Bible School) and the Institute Biblique Bethel (a Bible Institute on the secondary and post-secondary levels). The Institute opened only recently at the site of the TEE center in Libreville as a result of TEE students wishing to accelerate their studies to full-time, and also become full-time pastors. This may be the first time a TEE program started a residence program!

Aim of the Program

The aim of ETD-Gabon is to bring people into conformity to Christ's image and to mobilize the church and train its members to do the work of the ministry. The pathway to this goal is evangelism, conversion, basic teaching, water baptism, a meaningful local church relationship, and systematic and progressive training (Fehr 1989, 2-3).

ETD focuses on the development of lay leadership for church planting. The Christians of Gabon are part of a mobile society. They are constantly being moved to new places as their employers see fit. ETD-Gabon attempts to turn that fact into an asset by equipping them, so that when they go to new places they can contribute to the church, or if there is no church, they can begin one through a prayer cell and Bible study. Churches who "lose" such people are encouraged to pray for them as they go, that they will start new churches. The director of ETD calls them "sent laypeople" (Fehr 1989, 9).

ETD has gained great credibility with the church because it is helping to expand the church and plant new ones, while at the same time it is non-threatening to the church leadership. ETD lets the students know that they are striving, not for ordination, but to be the best possible servants of God. If students do get a call to the ministry, they are well prepared to enter full-time study.

Ephesians 4:13 summarizes the aim and philosophy of this program: "Until we all reach unity in the faith and in the knowledge of the Son of God and become mature, attaining to the whole measure of the fullness of Christ (NIV)." It demonstrates that Christians, though in the secular world, can be dedicated servants of God, as fully active in the church as pastors.

I asked a young couple, both involved in C&MA's ETD program, how they felt about TEE. They responded, "It is a good way to help people serve the Lord, to train them, and give them greater maturity and responsibility." What better way is there to say, "equip the saints for ministry."

Administration

ETD-Gabon operates like a school but has nonformal functions. The head of the program is called the director. The success of this program lies in the intangible—the zeal and insight of its director, Julie Fehr. When I asked the question "What makes TEE tick in Gabon?" the reply was, "We will tell you—Julie Fehr!" Her enthusiasm is contagious. Fehr works out of a central office, which for eight years was in her apartment, but now is located in an office/school complex purchased by the C&MA in Libreville.

ETD-Gabon is divided into eight districts, each with a coordinator responsible to the director. 75 tutors (15 missionary/60 national) work under the district coordinators. All are well trained, and "if no one is qualified to lead a TEE class, then (there is) no TEE." ETD presently registers 350 students.

Coordinators

The coordinator may be a missionary, or one who has developed through the program from student to class leader. The work is done on a volunteer status, without subsidy.

Coordinators deal with the central office, do paperwork, and give out report cards and certificates. They get books from the Alliance Book Stores and distribute them to the tutors. They work with the tutors to arrange for courses and schedules at the beginning of each term and have the big job of integrating the students' practical work with the local churches.

Coordinators meet with their tutors every few months for training sessions. Since they are local, they are always available for help during the week. They supervise classes and may pop in at any time to evaluate. When present in class they make on-the-spot suggestions, sometimes intervening in the class. A coordinator may be a teacher as well, as the need presents itself.

John Bouma, a coordinator, is responsible for arranging classes in his church. Two classes are doing Discipleship Level, one having started two years before the other. He is also responsible for arrangements for the advanced Servant Level.

National Leadership

The whole ETD works with a Theological Training Committee composed of the national church president, the mission director, two pastors chosen from year to year, a Gabonaise financial secretary, the TEE director, and the Bible Institute director. A definite mission-church partnership makes the system cohere.

The missionaries work hard on developing national leadership. Fehr's dream was that ETD should have been nationalized in five years. The church refused to appoint a national to be ETD director because they didn't have one who was qualified (with an M.A. from a graduate school). The one who is in training for this position is leading, as shepherding elder, a local church. He will shortly be installed as director of ETD, taking missionary Fehr's place.

I interviewed a young national, Emmanuel Mamboundou, who was prepared to take over the work of Roland Bowman, a missionary serving as coordinator in the Port Gentil area. Mamboundou feels it will be difficult to fill Bowman's shoes. "And who am I going to pass the buck to," he jokes, "now that Bowman is gone?" But in all seriousness he is prepared in heart and mind to work in collaboration with the pastors for ETD. He senses the prayer support surrounding him as he assumes this position.

Record Keeping

Well-kept records fill the adequate cabinet space. The records of all students are stored here according to the area in which they are currently studying. Duplicate records are stored by tutors in local churches.

Resident Bible Schools

TEE in Gabon has a residence school operating alongside both levels of its ETD program. The Ecole Biblique Bethel coordinates with the ETD Discipleship Level. Credit is given between these two schools, and students may transfer from one to the other. The TEE program requires service in the local church throughout its studies. The Ecole Biblique requires two years of residence training and two years of acceptable ministry before going on to the TEE advanced Servant Level.

The ETD Servant Level and the Institute Biblique Bethel with which it coordinates are advanced level programs. The Institute offers a 2-1-2 program: two years of Bible education in the Ecole Biblique, or the 15 courses of the ETD Discipleship Level, or the first two years at the Institute Biblique (which equates with the two-year program at the Ecole Biblique and ETD Discipleship Level); plus one year of acceptable ministry; which qualifies the student for the final two years of advanced study at the Institute Biblique. Students from TEE can cross over to residence, or vice versa. This program was developed in the hope that it would turn out more highly educated pastors.

A certain leader completed the 15 courses of the ETD Discipleship Level. So thorough was his training and so effective his service during those years, that both the people and the church leadership felt confidence in his ministry. He was granted the right to baptize as pastor in the church he will serve for two years. After that he plans to pastor his former home church. He will no doubt have opportunity there to continue his studies on the Servant Level.

TEE and Church Planting

TEE closely intertwines with church planting in the C&MA national church of Gabon. The Lambarene Church is only three years old. Prior to the coming of a missionary, TEE students were there, working for the power and light company and some major government agencies. They began developing a local church.

Later, Bowman visited the area and noted their work. When a permanent missionary came, he initiated TEE courses, strengthening the leaders. One of these leaders is now being transferred to Mula, where there is a church, but no TEE class. His input will be to start a new TEE class, a growth-inducing, stabilizing influence for the church.

In another area, believers who were transferred invited missionaries to come and hold a weekend seminar on TEE. One of the more experienced couples subsequently began TEE classes, establishing the church.

At Movanda, a rural area, believers from the Congo were employed at a sugar refinery. They began a church with some local people in the area. Laypeople who transferred in started a TEE class with the help of a missionary. Since the missionary had to work in other areas periodically, the people learned to lead the church themselves as part of their practical work in TEE. Of the 200-300 believers, all the literate leadership is trained through TEE.

The pattern of TEE students helping to plant a church and the TEE class helping to develop leadership in the church has aided the growth of the C&MA in Gabon. This comes about as a result of a deliberate policy to "consider the neighborhood Bible study or the prayer cell begun by the TEE student as a base for planting an evangelical church" (Fehr 1989, 7).

Component Parts

ETD-Gabon insists that the student gain theoretical knowledge, but just as strongly insists that the student practice such knowledge as soon as he acquires it, by serving the Lord in a regular ministry (Fehr 1989, 6). Such an orientation affects each component part in the TEE model.

Type of Student

Three years after the beginning of the ETD program, the leaders did a profile of their students. The students represented many professions: nurses, masons, builders, mechanics, business people, accountants, health workers, teachers, engineers, and housewives, to name a few. Most of these, 52 out of 84 (86%), had known the Lord for less than five years (Profile 1983, 2). By 1989, 53 different occupations were listed for TEE students. The program's emphasis on new lay leadership was in full swing.

TEE books are attractively displayed in the churches. When people inquire about buying them, they are introduced to the TEE training courses. Many enroll. TEE students are laypeople whose imagination has been stirred and their intellectual and spiritual curiosity aroused, to study the Word of God.

Originally one pastor had an upwardly mobile congregation of young members with good jobs and incomes. Not intimidated by their higher social level, this wise man integrated them into his church and encouraged them to study. He invited Fehr to his home, where he had gathered about twenty businessmen, schoolteachers, nurses, and others, so she could introduce them to TEE. By January of 1980, the first solid core of TEE trainees was studying.

TEE students are both older and younger people gifted by the Spirit for service. One of Bowman's first TEE students is now the coordinator of the huge 3000 member Avia-II C&MA church in Libreville. At Ntoume, the Lord has used a layman to plant churches wherever he goes. It seems that every few years this man is transferred to an area which has no church. Using the skills he learned in TEE, he establishes a new work.

Self-Study Material

ETD-Gabon uses the AEAM Text-Africa programmed books in both their Discipleship and Servant Levels. Teachers feel the books are well structured and organized. They are contextualized so that a student, no matter what level of education he has, deals with a lesson from which he can get good, solid teaching. By reading the Bible and doing the lesson day by day, the discipline of a devotional pattern is developed. French copies of the Text-Africa series are ordered from Cote d'Ivoire.

The curriculum is filled out with additional courses. By using other than programmed texts, the leaders believe students will be better prepared for possible residence study. Among those in use are Evangelism Explosion's material—dividing it into two 10-week courses to follow *Bringing People to Jesus* (Moyo and Holland 1973), Child Evangelism Fellowship's teacher training courses, and SEAN materials from England. Supplement sheets and articles are used in some of the courses.

Fehr told me that the C&MA leaders also want to produce some of their own programmed courses. They are holding training courses for ten writing teams from the six C&MA francophone countries in Africa, giving instruction in programmed writing. They aim to produce programmed texts for the training of TEE tutors, on missions and church history. A C&MA writers' team in Burkina Faso has the church history text in progress.

ETD-Gabon produces an "illustrated TEE" publication, based on the AEAM series, for illiterate and semiliterate students. The key lesson is written out in a few short sentences, using easy words and lots of space, with a line drawing which pictures the lesson. Each lesson coordinates with the Text-Africa lesson. Students take part in discussion and repeat the material orally for exam purposes.

Most of the AEAM series have contextualized stories illustrating the lesson. A criticism surfaced that some of the books are heavy on text but light on stories, which are so apropos for Africa and from which spiritual principles can be deduced. Books written for Africa need to contain types of instruction appropriate for cultures in which oral instruction dominates.

It is important that stories illustrative of spiritual principles are embodied in the book because the self-teaching manual, not the class leader, is the teacher. It therefore behooves writers of TEE material to include everything that makes for good teaching. The tutor can overcome this intermittent lack of stories by asking for additional real life illustrations of the lessons in the discussion seminar.

Service in the Church

TEE challenges students to improve in their Christian life and equips them for the work of the ministry, says Moussounda Nzigou, a tutor. A young married man told us, "The practical application is the hardest part of TEE. They ask us to do hard things—lead a group or lead a prayer cell."

Practical work requires the student to express the central truth of the lesson in a given assignment. When the class meets the following week, students report how the assignment went. Some teachers, such as David Bill and Mamboundou, require a written report of the practical assignment each week. Testimonies abound from these accounts.

Assignments take many forms. Students in the evangelism course share their faith with another person. In Libreville 25 prayer cells meet each week and TEE students lead many of these. Women use their practical assignments among the other women.

Germaine, one such student, does her practical assignments in her women's group and brings a report to class. Women also preach (in the women's conference). Their preaching is of such high calibre, the church president, Bakoukou, compares it as equivalent to or better than the evangelists and pastors.

Because churches are so understaffed, the local church has more and more work for TEE students to do. When a pastor is present, the practical work done by TEE students multiplies his effectiveness. Bakoukou points out that when others see laypeople walking with the Lord, they can identify with them. "There is an impact in the marketplace . . . Where the pastor cannot necessarily make an impact, laypeople can. Also, there are more of them. The pastor is only one. But because the workers have multiplied, so have the number of people who are contacted."

The ETD is so arranged that by the time students do their third or fourth course, they are becoming more and more involved in the local church. They minister increasingly throughout their course of study. Service by the participants in TEE is one of the strongest aspects of the program.

Discussion Seminars

Each class begins with a check to see that the lesson material is understood. This is followed by a written quiz. Students are graded on the quiz, and on whether or not they have filled out their books, said their verses, and done their practical work. Discussion develops from the report back on practical work and carries over into discussion of the new lesson.

John Bouma gave ETD tutor training to students at the newly begun (1989) Institute Biblique Bethel. They expressed amazement at the TEE method of discussion, so different from the French lecture system in their earlier student experiences. The idea of learning from the text, then sharing and discussing the lesson as a means of instruction, stimulated their interest.

Clement, a mature Christian in the church, has been both a TEE student and tutor. It delights him to know that students can become teachers and still continue to learn. We all learn as we go forward in growth and knowledge throughout life. Yet all teach, too, because we all share experience and insight in the discussion seminars. It is nice to know, he said, that in the Body of Christ, we participate in these experiences together. This distinctly Christian point of view opposes the philosophies of esoteric knowledge embodied in many tribal religions.

Tutors

Tutors, called "responsables" in French, take responsibility for the conduct of the discussion class. ETD tutors are lay leaders, with the exception of a few pastors who have taken tutor training.

ETD-Gabon focuses on the challenge of training sufficient personnel for this volunteer post. Some churches in the interior want TEE classes but cannot have them for lack of a trained tutor. Students at the Bible School and Institute take TEE tutor training. An apprenticeship program helps channel students into tutor training. Samuel was one such tutor. A student for two years, he was tapped for apprenticeship. He moved on to leading classes on the "buddy" system, and now, after four years, leads his own classes. The apprenticeship system drew him into the role of a full-fledged tutor.

Tutors watch students who show interest and capability carefully for their potential. When they complete five to ten courses (about two years), they may be asked to help as unofficial assistants to the tutor. First duties include taking attendance, collecting fees, and listening to verses. As they become accustomed to the system and do well, they may advance to the mature duties of an official aid, such as leading a discussion class.

Tutors agree that preparation for a discussion class is one of their biggest jobs and entails considerable reading. Future tutors need to be discipled into thorough preparation for something as important to TEE as the discussion seminar. If they show gifts for the work, and their home and life are in order, they may take the tutor training course. When they complete the course and have been checked by a coordinator, they teach their own classes. After they serve in the program for four years, tutors receive a book bag with the insignia of the Alliance Church on it as a symbol of faithfulness.

Tutor Training

ETD-Gabon offers a tutor training course both to students at the Bible School and Institute, and to students who have come up through the ranks as assistants. They use as textbook the well known basic monograph written by Fred Holland, *Teaching Through TEE* (1975). A workbook, called "Formacion" in French, goes along with Holland's work. Each trainee must read the text, fill out the workbook, and attend six weeks of discussion classes.

The course is very detailed including lessons on how to organize a TEE class, fill out and use all the administrative forms (on which they are specifically tested), conduct classes, and lead discussion. After successfully completing the course, students meet with the coordinator and the church education committee for examination. If pronounced fit, they are ready for a class of their own.

The goal is to use local people as quickly as possible on the Discipleship Level, so missionaries and key national leaders can offer courses on the Servant Level for those who meet the requirements. Tutors continue to study, completing Discipleship and going on to Servant Level, which makes them very busy people.

Evaluation is part of the in-service training for all involved in TEE. Toward the end of each semester (three semesters each year), a weekend refresher course is held in each region for all coordinators, tutors, and assistant tutors. This includes time for discussion and evaluation of the semester just drawing to a close and going over plans for the coming semester.

Spiritual Foundation

The aim of the Alliance Church TEE program—to be made into the image of Christ—certainly reveals a spiritual foundation. One aspect of this foundation is the desire to study and serve the Lord.

Clement 'Allogo testified that his desire to serve the Lord came when he attended a service in a C&MA church in Libreville where report cards were being given out to TEE students. He came from another denomination and couldn't study. In his words, "I hid the desire away in my heart and said if I ever get the chance, that's what I want to do. I want to know God's Word, and study it the way those people are studying God's Word." Clement joined the C&MA and enrolled in TEE classes. He enjoys his study now in Port Gentil and works faithfully in the church. Such deep desires reveal a spiritual foundation.

Another student tells that when he heard Bowman was going to begin TEE classes in his area, he "jumped at the chance." He attended classes every semester and now assists the leader.

The spiritual foundation includes motivated students whose desires have been touched by the Holy Spirit. One man expressed his desire in these words: "Now that I have gotten into the meat of the Word, I really have a hunger to go on and find out what the rest is about too." Many TEE students want to go on for further training. They have been stimulated in the Word of God and want to complete their studies for full-time service.

External Relationships

In 1979 when TEE first began with pastors, it didn't seem to work. They simply said, "We've all finished Bible School. Why should we take courses?" But in 1980-81 when Christian lay leaders began to study, the idea took hold. Even the older pastors unaccustomed to, or unacquainted with, the TEE system accepted it for their people. It sparked the whole church to revival and involved increasing numbers of lay leaders.

Now the C&MA TEE program has the full acceptance and endorsement of the church. A close working relationship exists between the church and the missionaries. This harmony led to unusual cooperation and advancement of both TEE and the church as an expression of partnership.

I had a superb interview with Bakoukou, the head administrator of the Alliance Church in Gabon. He has a firm conviction, based on his experience, that TEE helps the church. He believes without hesitation or qualification that the church accepts TEE—not only accepts it, but wants it in operation everywhere.

Many who come to the Lord are now led to the Lord by TEE students. All through the week people led to the Lord by the TEE participants will be brought to the pastor. This happens constantly through the week so that the Sunday morning service is not the main event of the week anymore. In the prayer cells, frequently led by extension personnel, people find the Lord and are discipled, with extension students acting as shepherds.

A future goal of the church for TEE is that it should begin to receive college credit for its higher level.

Problems

Gabon is a very mobile society. This, one would think, creates problems of continuity in courses and curriculum. But ETD turned this, its number one problem, into a blessing. The program has used TEE students as church planters, and TEE classes as nurture and discipling tools for new areas.

The second problem concerns time. Louise, a coordinator, confesses that she cannot find time to do all the administrative work. A class leader reports that in order to master the lesson he must take time to read and prepare for the discussion. A coordinator (who may become the national director) explains that his work as coordinator is not a full-time ministry, so he carefully schedules time between his personal work and the work of the Lord. Considering that lay people work at secular jobs and other church activities, extension presents a challenge due to the pressure of time.

Students also have a problem with time and too many things to do. When there is just not enough time to do everything, it may be TEE that gets dropped. There is perhaps a 10-20% attrition rate during the first 15 courses of the Discipleship Level. The director feels that some drop out due to activities such as leading a prayer cell. Others take "time out" to absorb what they are learning and return to the program. Some feel they cannot invest the time, and others are spiritually lazy. For whatever reasons, due to the pressure of time, some just give up and drop their studies mid-course.

Innovations

TEE is a strong enough system that it can be pushed into different molds, be bettered by it, and succeed.

C&MA's willingness to expand the curriculum and include other types of courses marks the kind of integration TEE programs need. It avoids exclusivism and will be a continuing force in Africa. By integrating courses like Evangelism Explosion and Child Evangelism Fellowship, Gabon TEE avoids a seriously confusing situation in which good evangelical programs are placed in competition with one another. TEE is not in competition with these programs; it can assimilate and be strengthened by them.

For example, CEF missionary Becky DeBerry has adapted the whole French CEF program into ten weeks of classes, which fits into the TEE schedule. Pedagogy is one area of specialization in the overall ETD curriculum. Anyone who does the Child Evangelism Fellowship training receives credit from TEE toward their certificate. The whole point, Fehr explained, is that the people are trained better for ministry.

Another out-of-the-ordinary adjustment is that in areas which are difficult to reach, the tutor goes once a month and does three or four classes (covering a week's lesson in each class) *in one weekend*. Thus the ten weeks of lessons can be completed on time though the tutor cannot reach the area each week.

Most take the TEE courses in French. Some however have limited reading ability and ETD has developed what they call "Illustrated TEE." Workbooks created parallel to an AEAM programmed book use pictures which summarize each day's lesson. The pictures are simple line drawings. One or two sentences of text summarize the lesson. Lesson time for those using Illustrated TEE includes lecture and filling in the lesson; problems are discussed as they arise.

Semiliterate or illiterate students are able to explain the lessons and participate in study. This is one of the most exciting innovations in TEE in Africa.

Esther Bibili, a leader among the women of the Alliance Church, produced five of these books, much in demand. She devises the pictures herself and selects the written text, using a minimum of printed words. Esther has herself completed 30 TEE courses. She asked Julie Fehr one day if anyone prays for those who write the programmed books. "How do they know what to write?" she asks in amazement. She especially prays for the writers of the Text-Africa series.

One special innovation of ETD utilizes the mobility of their society to plant churches. TEE students and tutors transferred from one area are encouraged to begin a prayer cell in their new area until a TEE class can be formed. As the TEE students witness and lead some to Christ, a local church begins. This has developed into a pattern. New churches have been planted in many areas of Gabon.

Blessings

Several items illuminate the success and blessing of the Alliance church's TEE program. The involvement of 99% of C&MA's local churches, plus the interest of people in other churches, demonstrate that TEE has been a blessing. They have had increasing growth in the quantity and quality of students since 1980. Figures showing 84 students in 1983 and 350 students in 1990 represent 400% growth in seven years.

The desire to study the Word of God and the resultant Christian growth is in itself a blessing.

Helena says that the Word is like a mirror revealing habits and practices (as wrong). She thanks the Lord for what He has done in changing her life style.

A choir leader, transferred to an area where there was no pastor, realized his inability to explain the Bible when he needed to assume pastoral roles. In due time he was transferred once more, this time to an area where they had TEE. He immediately began to study, deeply grateful for what he is learning. His only regret is that he didn't start sooner.

Another testifies that before she began training she was not able to help other Christians with their problems. Since studying in TEE she can come up with spiritual solutions.

One Christian, a mason who helped the mission build several buildings, began studying through TEE. Even though lacking in some educational qualifications, this man has been used to start two churches. Now he wants to go to Bible school. Home study gave him an overwhelming desire to serve the Lord as a pastor.

Another by-product of the TEE classes has been the fact that women and minorities have reached fulfillment through their study and contribute greatly to the life of the church. The president of the church indicated that it raised the level of the underprivileged and those "who have been left out" or filled no major role in church life. In fact, the whole level of the church's understanding has been raised, and he claims they have a different quality of Christian now. Students use their studies as a basis for communicating to people. They actually do the things they learn in the TEE books—how to pray, teach, witness, and live varied facets of the Christian life.

A great blessing has been the desire of Christians from the Congo, who started their own church in 1982, to study the Word. Roland Bowman, a regional director in Gabon, received a request from Congo in 1988 to come help them.

He had a formidable task: to disciple a group of 2500 Christians. Missionaries are not allowed to stay in this Marxist country. They are only permitted very brief visits. Bowman decided, despite the shortness of time he was permitted to be in the country, to begin a TEE program to train national Congolese leaders in effective discipleship methods. It prospered despite the necessarily short introductory course.

On one weekend, Bowman literally explained how TEE worked, prepped class leaders (tutors), and went through a lesson in the books to demonstrate how it worked. He instructed them on how to do the homework assignments, memory work, quizzes, and practical service. He taught them what he could in the time available about discussion classes. Then he returned to Gabon.

Now these dear people, who had never before done TEE, began to have classes. None of them had ever seen a TEE class, except as simulated by Bowman that weekend. After three months, Bowman secured permission for another weekend visit and returned to the Congo. He found the students had completed their books, had had a great time in the discussion classes, and were ready for the final test. While Bowman admits this was a very unorthodox way to begin TEE, it worked. He now has 12 trained tutors (with 8 more in training) holding classes for 80 church leaders in Congo.

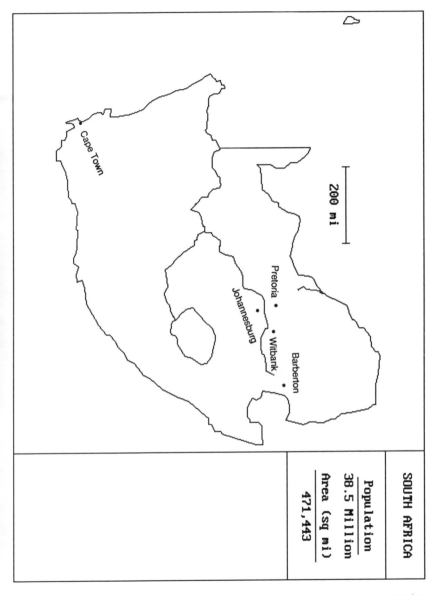

SOUTH AFRICA

Population
38.5 Million

Area (sq mi)
471,443

200 mi

Cape Town

Pretoria

Johannesburg

Witbank

Barberton

CHAPTER TEN

From Witbank to Barberton

The room was crowded, and eager faces turned toward Mrs. Anita Johnson, a missionary from Sweden, as she exhorted them on the importance of training through TEE. Johnson had no previous experience in TEE when she took charge of the second largest TEE program in South Africa, Phumelela Bible School Extension (PSBSE). The program had grown so big it could not keep track of its classes.

Seeking to prepare herself for the task ahead, she sought out instruction from a missionary well schooled in TEE, and from Moses Nkosi, former assistant principal of the program. She took a class herself as a student to see what it looked like from the "inside" and attended the TEE seminar held regularly for leaders of the program. Then she took up the threads and began to lead the school.

Missionary Stig Bergman began the school in 1975-76 for the Alliance denomination, daughter church to the Swedish Alliance Mission. The church and mission have amalgamated—missionaries and nationals are both part of the Alliance Church—which gives a great sense of oneness to the TEE program. Olaf Hjelmefiord (principal) and Nkosi (assistant principal) developed TEE from 1976 to 1985, years of fast growth. Jan Gustafson led from 1986 to 1988; Johnson took leadership in 1989-1990 and turned over the reins to Jim Skosana in 1991.

The largest TEE school in South Africa is the Theological Education by Extension College (TEEC) of Johannesburg, an interdenominational program reporting over 700 students in 1986 (Hughes 1990, 28). Phumelela follows next in line with 620 students, the largest denominational program in that country.

Aim of the Program

The aim of Phumelela Bible School Extension of the Alliance Church of South Africa is to equip all local church leaders. The principal, Skosana, specifically stressed development of disciples and of lay leadership as his two foremost aims in the administrator's questionnaire. He feels this aim is "greatly fulfilled." With 65 tutors, 80 classes, and 620 active students, the evidence supports his claim.

The aim of the program is strengthened by the fact that church policy states "every church must have a TEE school" and "every leader must take TEE courses." The philosophy underlying this aim was expressed a number of times in interdenominational workshops which I held with Hjelmefiord. He firmly believed that each church should be a Bible school, and every pastor a Bible teacher who trains his leaders (Hjelmefiord 1989, 6).

In an address to tutors and other church leaders at a training session, Skosana asked the penetrating, goal-oriented question, "Where are we going?" He answered it by comparing those who study via TEE with those who do not. Those who study the Bible through TEE evidence growth toward maturity. Whenever Skosana visits a church to preach and promote TEE, he gains more students and sees growth and improvement in the program. This is his goal, and one he would like to see continue to succeed.

In summary, the aim of PBSE is that church leaders study the Word of God to learn to function as leaders and mature Christians.

Administration

The PBSE program fills important nonformal functions, but nevertheless uses a formal school-linked title—principal—to denote its director. The principal is responsible to the church aided by a corps of willing pastors. The pastors of the Alliance Church stand behind the TEE program and are readily available to assist as needed.

The church conference appoints the principal, assistant principal, and a TEE committee. In addition each church chooses its own TEE committee locally. The director oversees the work of the school, liaisons with the churches, plans for the training of tutors, orders books, and keeps all office records. The Swedish Alliance Mission provides a spacious office to keep detailed and accurate records of all students, courses, fees, attendance, grades, and work assignments.

Records of all who received certificates and diplomas are neatly and carefully set out in loose leaf binders.

The basic level TEE consists of 14 courses, with an advanced level of 12 additional courses. Students receive a certificate for each individual course completed, and diplomas for completion of the basic and the advanced level. Award ceremonies are held each year in local churches to recognize students and present them with certificates and diplomas. 978 course certificates have been given out in its fourteen-year history, and 150 basic course diplomas.

One year's credit is given in the denomination's Bible College for completion of the basic 14 TEE courses, but accreditation is not emphasized. Most work of the program is done on the basic level. The nonformal aim of TEE—developing leadership skills—is the focus.

Johnson appointed a key contact in each church and used him as assistant in keeping communications regarding TEE going with the church. She sent regular reminders to the key contact, specifically a sheet called "How to Walk the TEE Road," with instruction on such items as how to start a class, duties of the tutor, training tips—all to keep the church alerted to TEE.

Component Parts

Examining the component parts of TEE gives a basis for comparison and analysis of the case studies in this book.

Type of students

A list of those who study includes house-cell leaders (prayer groups), (local church) committee members, all church workers, all who lead services (including men's and women's group leaders), Sunday school teachers, evangelists, and pastors. Most are mature leaders, although young people are welcomed. The program stresses getting the right students with good aims and study habits.

Students know where they are headed and try to keep up with the work of filling in their programmed texts and doing practical assignments. Tutors are told that if students begin well but drop off, they should be asked to testify as to what they are receiving and asked to do more practical service. Last year the administration of PBSE gave attention to "waking up sleepy TEE classes" with this renewed emphasis on testimony and practical service.

Self-Study Material

Phumelela uses only the AEAM programmed texts. It has been active in the Nguni Language Text Committee, which helps get the Text-Africa books translated into the vernacular. The Alliance Church has so far sponsored the translation and publication of eight books. (The Free Methodist Church, Wesleyan Church, Africa Evangelical Fellowship, and The Evangelical Alliance Mission have also contributed to the production of twenty-one Zulu translations of the AEAM Text-Africa series).

A university student said she appreciated the books because she felt she was learning on a college level. The deeper meaning of the Bible and its message were being taught through the information given in the programmed texts. Time for study was not a problem for her, even though she was a busy wife and mother, because each day's lesson "takes only 15-20 minutes to complete."

In a seminar I attended, one of the tutors was able to give an "off the cuff" synopsis of each of the 14 books in the curriculum. Respect for the programmed books as aids to Bible study was evident. The Alliance Church subsidizes the texts so that all pay the same price for English (about $3) and Zulu (about $2.50) texts.

Service in the Church

Since the denomination requires all local church leaders to attend TEE classes, this builds the service of the student into the program in most instances. Those who serve in the church become PBSE students, and they continue and expand their service. TEE provides focus and training for that service.

Elias testifies that studying helped him do soul winning. Jan says that TEE helped him improve both his prayer life and his preaching. Esther stated that extension helped her organize her sermons better.

Fifty percent of an available group of twenty TEE students claim they led people to Christ in the last two years. A total of 25 people were won to Christ through the efforts of these ten students. They brought fourteen people into their churches.

The remaining fifty percent, who led no one to the Lord in the last two years, represent a group within PBSE who do not easily implement the training they get in class. Some study for inward growth and knowledge and are not as apt to do evangelism. "Most of our students are eager to witness, lead Bible studies, and counsel other believers," asserts Skosana. "And while they develop discipling skills, they help the health of the whole church" (1991).

TEE students do many things to lighten the pastor's load. They lead small groups, preach, and witness. Pastor Nkosi related to me that his church is especially blessed when TEE students lead services, testify, and preach (1990).

Discussion Seminars

In the class I observed, students completed their programmed lesson and there was good interaction. As a visitor and author of three AEAM programmed texts, I was an object of some curiosity, and students wanted to ask me questions. Nevertheless, the discussion reflected interaction on previous class topics and evidenced sufficient give-and-take among class members. I perceived good rapport and eagerness to share.

Students revealed that as their group had been together a long time, they were not afraid to share with one another. Problem-solving takes place in the discussion—even problems not referred to in the text. Interaction takes place between the students, who seem ready to help one another. Everyone gets a chance to talk.

Some felt that at times discussion stays too long on one topic. If the leader is not alert and fails to move discussion forward to other topics, time is used up and other pertinent discussion must be tabled.

In some classes discussion of the lesson and application become "hot." Students have a lot to say and the dialogical learning process is at work. Other classes, however, reflect the fact that neither leader nor students know what the discussion is supposed to accomplish. These need further training.

Skosana feels strongly that as the TEE students interact and share their thoughts in discussion, they grow in problem-solving ability. TEE is training them to think.

Tutors

The Phumelela school uses pastors, Bible school graduates, seasoned elders, and school teachers as tutors. The TEE Committee of each local church liaisons with the principal in their selection. Many are inexperienced in TEE and must be trained in discussion methods, administration, how to order books from headquarters, and how to fill out the necessary forms. This is done in regular training sessions.

Tutors must be trained to be responsible to encourage the students, because it is not easy for African students to study in the crowded conditions of their home. If the tutor takes things too lightly, he or she may not prepare for class as well as necessary, and students will notice this. If they sense an indifferent attitude, it sets a poor example. Tutors must have zeal for the class and guide it well.

Tutor Training

Tutor training is one of the strong points of Phumelela's program. They held seminars in each district as well as nationally and developed a compendium for use in training discussion group leaders. Six training seminars were held in 1990 and four in the first half of 1991 in widely scattered areas from Witbank to Barberton.

One that I attended had six national leaders plus the principal in charge of various training sessions. They divided into three working groups: one (for new tutors) teaching the basics of TEE methods; one discussing ways and means to instruct pastors who lack understanding of TEE and are unaware of the benefits it brings to the church; and one on how to improve the functioning of a TEE class and inspire zeal. Ten people wanted to start TEE classes in their district. They stayed afterward for a time to organize them.

Basic TEE workshops train tutors to:

1. Lead discussion.
2. Register students and take attendance.
3. Pay for books against an invoice as soon as possible. PBSE keeps all the AEAM programmed books at one price.
4. Order testpapers in Week Eight of the course.
5. Order new books at headquarters for the next term also during Week Eight, using the order list.
6. Return tests to headquarters for correction with the attendance list. Test results are registered in the TEE file for classes.
7. Receive the list of grades, certificates, and diplomas.

Spiritual Foundation

PBSE has strong spiritual aims. The Alliance Church places much emphasis on prayer and the work of the Holy Spirit in their doctrine, and therefore in their TEE program as well. They carefully monitor the spiritual qualifications of tutors. Prayer time before class helps to deepen the spiritual base. The discussions lead to spiritual insights.

Johnson points to the growth of both the church and TEE. Additional classes have begun. In Witbank, coal mining center of South Africa, the Alliance Church holds five classes instead of one or two. Besides lively classes and students full of zeal, the spiritual foundation is evident and the Holy Spirit is at work. The program relates very closely to the church and the spark of revival grows.

External Relationships

The church as a whole clearly approves of the program. Many TEE programs across Africa struggle to gain pastoral acceptance, but not this one. Nevertheless, despite the fact that denominational policy calls for every church to have TEE classes, the message has not reached some outlying churches. A plan has been devised for contact persons in each district to awaken such churches. The contact person, being on the spot, liaisons with the principal to explain TEE to these pastors, how it can help their church, and encourage active participation.

Problems

The problem of keeping track of classes because of geographical distance and keeping church people informed creates a major problem in PBSE. For this reason a key contact person was appointed for each church, as a bridge between office and class. Some classes slow down when the principal is unable to visit them. The key contact person especially helps these churches.

Contact Persons

The TEE contact person (usually a pastor, deacon, or elder) works with a committee in every church to see that the work goes forward. His job description was spelled out by the church in a paper distributed to all at a training seminar. His duties are to:

1. Work with the TEE Committee toward the goal of having all leaders in the church study the Word, and to function as members and mature Christians. Home cells are to be encouraged in churches with TEE.

2. Know of all activities concerning TEE in the district: number of classes and students, how well they function, and what help is needed from the home office.

3. Communicate with the central TEE office prior to church district meetings for any announcements or proposed changes in the program and report back to the TEE office after every church district meeting.

4. Visit TEE groups and train tutors in their administrative responsibilities.

5. Call the TEE office for problem solving, encouragement, training seminars and graduation plans. The contact person arranges the meetings and contacts all organizations and churches for the meeting.

6. Be a bridge between the TEE office and the local group especially in problem areas.

7. Arrange with class leaders for award ceremonies to be held during Sunday morning services. This not only encourages the student, but also draws others into the class. Ask for a freewill offering for TEE at that service and send it to the TEE office via the church treasurer.

Lack of Understanding TEE

Some pastors do not understand TEE. This hinders the growth of classes. A working group was created at a training seminar to help such pastors learn what TEE can do for their church. The group resolved that the first point of importance would be to share with pastors that their ministries would be enhanced by TEE students. In fact, helping the pastor is a criteria by which the success of TEE is judged. They outlined four things pastors need to know and do to understand TEE.

1. TEE lightens the pastor's load because students help visit members, witness, lead services, and teach the Word.
2. Pastors should attend a seminar on TEE to see how it works.
3. TEE should be explained at the periodic ministers' meeting.
4. Leaders should talk to individual pastors and explicate the value of extension.

They also threw down a challenge to students to set a good example, and thereby make it easier to win their pastors. If fear or pride held them back from serving the Lord with the new skills they were learning in class, then their pastors also would be held back.

Difficulties with Fees

Transferral of funds is a difficulty in PBSE. When funds arrive late at the central office (or not at all), the program slows down and effectiveness drops. Faithfulness in handling of fees and finances becomes both an administrative and a moral challenge which class leaders must face.

Innovations

The Alliance Church requires all its elected or appointed leaders in any phase of church work to take TEE classes. This innovation represents one way of guaranteeing clientele for the program.

A second innovation worth noting is that Phumelela sets one price for all their books. This keeps inflation from preventing study. Of course, this means that the school subsidizes the books. On the other hand, the people support the program and give generously to church offerings and special offerings for TEE.

The introduction of a key contact person into the program is yet another innovation. The job description differs from that of coordinators and supervisors who train tutors and attend to administrative duties in the COCIN program. The contact person adds public relations for TEE to his duties.

Evaluation

Skosana views the future prospects of the Phumelela program as good. The people see the blessing of it and support it. The leaders of the church are studying, but these students form only a portion of the church. Other church members not yet leaders need to begin to study in TEE. They represent the potential students of the future. More are being encouraged to join classes. There is room for growth.

TEE students grow in ability to think and solve problems as they study through TEE. This carries over into other facets of their lives. They mature and interact with both church and community more confidently and objectively.

CHAPTER ELEVEN

Case Study
Summary and Comparisons

"A field mouse is known by its stripes," the Sotho people say. Each case study reveals a program with its own unique characteristics discovered in research. Tables 11.1-11.8 give a summary of their differences and commonalities in the following order: aims, administration, component parts, external relationships, problems, innovations, and how each program evaluates itself.

Table 11.1

Comparison of Aims

CECA Zaire	Both pastors and people attend TEE classes, the primary aim being the training of those already in ministry, but all Christians are included.
BEE Kenya	Original goal of pastoral training was not fulfilled; switched to lay leader training.
COCIN Nigeria	Began program as training for evangelists and succeeded; nevertheless opened the program to include training of laity to meet needs.
ETD Gabon	Uses aim of training leaders as a unique tool for church planting and ministry of Body.
PBSE South Africa	Aim is that all church leaders be trained through TEE, prerequisite to office.

The aims of each program should be carried out by an administration that is capable of performing efficiently enough to fulfill those aims. Note that regional coordinators form a bridge between directors and the classes, and have become an essential part of programs that are widespread geographically.

Table 11.2

Comparison of Patterns of Administration

CECA Zaire	Directors work with unpaid regional coordinators who administer the regions in a decentralized fashion.
BEE Kenya	National coordinator works from a central office with national BEE board; each region has a local BEE committee, and a regional coordinator who administers paperwork; has just turned over top leadership to national.
COCIN Nigeria	Director works from central office with translator, typist, bursar and storekeeper. Regional coordinators meet regularly with tutors, visit and assess classes, mark tests, and give grades; once paid—not currently; would like to revive stipend; national as principal for six years.
ETD Gabon	Director works from a central office; unpaid regional coordinators arrange course schedules with tutors and integrate practical work of students in local churches; missionary leads program but considering national director.
PBSE South Africa	Principal works from central office; has no regional coordinators; key contact persons appointed to assist in communications; national principal in for one year is facing transitional problems.

Table 11.3

Comparison of Record-Keeping, Course Requirements, and Awards

CECA Zaire	Principal and regional coordinators keep duplicate records; Bible school in one region keeps TEE records in its office. Does not give certificates to students but recognizes their attainments in local churches; gives certificates to tutors who go through training program. Students take courses as available.
BEE Kenya	Principal has redone all records since decentralization ended. Has 32 courses, 20 required and 12 electives. Awards certificates to tutors and students who meet basic requirements; tutors with three such are awarded colorful gold pin.
COCIN Nigeria	Director and coordinators keep meticulous records. Has three levels of six courses each (18) with an Advanced Program beyond that. Gives certificates for each level; does not give awards to tutors.
ETD Gabon	Director keeps meticulous records with regional coordinators keeping duplicates; 15 courses in Discipleship Level; 15 in Servant Level. Students receive diploma for each module; rewards apprentice tutors for completing 4 years with book bag embossed with church symbol.
PBSE South Africa	Principal keeps meticulous records; Basic module of 14 courses plus second module of 12. Gives students certificates for each course and module; does not give awards to tutors.

Table 11.4

Comparison of Component Parts

Type of student	CECA: many who lack higher education catered to in basic levels. BEE: many in lower educational levels trained; students must be in good standing with local church. COCIN: has lower and higher level programs; emphasizes laity and gifts. ETD-Gabon: has lower and higher level programs; many upwardly mobile career people young in the faith; leadership is target group, but all are welcome. PBSE: requires all church leaders to study; trains wide educational levels.
Self-study material	CECA: uses only AEAM programmed texts. BEE: BEE uses AEAM and other texts as well. COCIN: uses additional texts besides AEAM and has a few of its own TEE texts available for others. ETD-Gabon: uses AEAM; developing "illustrated TEE" from AEAM texts, using pictures for semi-literate; uses higher level books of various types in college level; has plans for writing teams. PBSE: uses only AEAM programmed texts.
Service in the church	In all studies participants were very active in evangelism, witnessing, church visiting, praying, helping pastors, leading services, teaching, and planting new churches.
Discussion Seminars	All indicate that the discussion greatly increases student understanding of the Bible and its application to daily life. A co-learner concept is emerging, giving rise to the ability to share one's point of view and use of Scripture to solve problems. Many classes have effective interaction; problems such as lecturing and reteaching the lesson occur.

Tutors	Tutors are the key to good discussion in all programs. Rapid expansion has sometimes led to use of unprepared tutors. CECA: frequently uses pastors; needs to develop skills in group dynamics. BEE: Sometimes uses tutors without TEE experience. COCIN: drafts tutors from among its students. ETD-Gabon: uses students in an apprenticeship model PBSE: sometimes uses inexperienced tutors.
Tutor Training	All 5 programs have workshops. CECA: trains tutors who have taken 2 or 3 TEE courses by enrolling them in special training. BEE: intensive training offered; debriefing sessions after they teach their first course. COCIN: regional coordinators meet weekly with tutors to go over the lesson methods to be used. ETD-Gabon: has special programmed tutor training course available to those completing 5 TEE courses; refresher course for evaluation at end of each term. PBSE: frequent comprehensive training seminars held regionally; have compendium for tutor use.
Spiritual Foundation	All programs share aim of spiritual formation, and have deeply motivated, spiritually hungry students who provide essential impetus for the whole program; many students show the fruit of changed lives, a desire to pray and read the Bible, and walk in the Spirit, evidences of true spiritual foundation.

How well a program handles the component parts is crucial in determining its level of success. Church approval is also another key dimension in all the case studies. Its importance cannot be overstressed. Note that acceptance and approval take a different form in each case.

Table 11.5

Comparison of Church Approval

CECA Zaire	Church owns program and is happy with it; desires its continuation; frustrated in its purpose to extend program due to lack of translated materials.
BEE Kenya	Jury is still out on full church approval; will be decided in future; some inertia may come from church reluctance to accept program.
COCIN Nigeria	Owned by the Church since inception; some uncertainty evidenced, perhaps, in lack of willingness to fund program.
ETD Gabon	Wholehearted approval has bred wide acceptance, though some pastors still lack understanding of program.
PBSE South Africa	Church adopted program as its own and requires TEE training for its leaders. Strong official approval.

Table 11.6

Comparison of Problems

CECA Zaire	Lack of books; lack of funding with inflation; lack of teacher transport.
BEE Kenya	Pastors (who lead classes) moved frequently; student self-discipline; lack of finances; rapid expansion; un-qualified tutors; and transitional issues.
COCIN Nigeria	Supervisor transport; lack of funding; transitional problems, student transfers.
ETD Gabon	A busy and mobile society takes students out in middle of term; lack of time for tutors and coordinators to do their jobs; need for national leader with continuing missionary assistance and support.
PBSE South Africa	Distance; lack of transport for the principal; lack of under-standing of the program.

Table 11.7

Comparison of Innovations

CECA Zaire	Use variety of methods; classes in remote areas are visited by tutor for 2 weeks of intensive training—students read and fill out workbooks in morning and have discussion in afternoon; a periodic 3-day tutor seminar is held on how to handle difficult theological problems arising in discussion classes.
BEE Kenya	Hold special refresher courses on subjects not in the AEAM series to bolster their curriculum; have new courses in pastoral and leadership skills; revamped their tutor training with renewed emphasis on importance of tutor.
COCIN Nigeria	Have two intermediary posts: regional directors (common to all but PBSE), and also a district supervisor with detailed duties spelled out specifically, truly integrating their program; write some of their own texts.
ETD Gabon	Use an expanded curriculum; devised "illustrated TEE" with simple line drawings for use with illiterate or semi-literate students; in remote areas, a tutor arrives for a weekend, holding intensive discussion classes to cover 3 or 4 weeks of study; best innovation is use of TEE students in church planting, viewing their training as development of church planting skills from the start.
PBSE South Africa	TEE *required* of *all* church leaders; sale of programmed texts at same price; use of a contact person for promoting TEE in local churches for public relations.

Table 11.8

How Each Case Study Evaluates Itself

CECA Zaire	Views itself as a program with positive values; develops skills in students; Bible study is deepened; students can answer questions about their faith; feels goal-fulfillment is hindered by financial problems and that runaway inflation dims future prospects.
BEE Kenya	Future ambiguous and dependent on full church approval; more pastors beginning classes in their churches; program needs watchful supervision; transition to national leadership is a crucial time; new leader needs encouragement.
COCIN Nigeria	Considers program a vital part of the church; has many testimonies of people growing spiritually and bearing fruit; leaders realize that church must decide whether to re-subsidize the coordinators to facilitate the program—if this problem is not resolved, a former director gives the program only a 50-50 chance of succeeding.
ETD- Gabon	With 99% church involvement and a 400% rate of student growth since 1983, prospects are bright for a good future; opening of neighboring Congo for TEE is astounding testimony as to how God used this program; turnover to national leadership is present critical point in progress.
PBSE South Africa	Believes future prospects are good; strength lies in stability and strong church approval; only dynamic leadership will pull program through testing days ahead.

Details and facets of each of these case studies teach us a variety of ways extension can be used to do the job of leadership training. Innovations with a wide range of creativity often alleviate problems. The variety of innovations also shows TEE as a flexible teaching model. Warnings come up like red flags which we must heed, adjusting our course of action.

I turn now to an integration of the findings of the case studies with the findings of the two questionnaires (chapters four and five) gaining an overall picture of the state of TEE in Africa.

Chapter Twelve

Data Analysis

What makes TEE tick? Why do some programs appear to succeed while others fail? What factors lead to effectiveness? This study confirms the three hypotheses stated in chapter one.

Hypothesis number one is that TEE is grounded in good educational theory. The principles of adult education and TEE clearly coordinate. TEE is a form of adult education and works because it embodies the essential precepts of this discipline. Principles of adult, continuing, nonformal, and distant education are exemplified in all five TEE case studies (chapters six through ten).

Hypothesis number two is that internal and external factors are identified and interrelated in the TEE model. The fact that program administrators responded to common questions on internal factors (component parts) and reported common data linking them with each other demonstrates that these internal factors are basic to the TEE model. The primary external relationship between the extension program and the denominational church sponsoring it is vital because all are church based.

Hypothesis number three is that effectiveness is dependent on rightly handling the component parts of TEE. The following data analysis confirms and elucidates important findings regarding this hypothesis.

Aims and Success

The aims of TEE programs in Africa center upon the development of local church leadership in the face of a paucity of trained grass roots leaders. Whether we use the less popular term "lay leadership" or "development of gifted, natural leaders," the focus remains on the *unordained* leadership. While some of these leaders may eventually be ordained, on-the-job training by TEE programs meets a great felt need for local church leadership on all ministry levels. Case studies and figures converge in their conclusions on this matter.

TEE programs succeed in that a high percentage of administrators report that their goals are being fulfilled (pages 67-68), although these goals must be sifted and refined by stakeholders (the church).

TEE inspires widespread evangelism, indicating a program alive and active. Each case study and the evidence of figures and percentages (chapter 5) confirm that evangelism is an important, if not *the* important, concern of TEE students.

TEE programs are often associated with church planting and church growth. Gabon-ETD, COCIN, and to some degree CECA correlate new church planting moves with TEE students. In thirty-eight out of seventy-eight programs (nearly 50%), administrators report that TEE students work in new church planting situations, with almost 100% involved in an established church. "Works in the church" tops the list of criteria for successful programs (page 66). Specifically, participants help the church in preaching, teaching, witnessing, leading services, and bringing people into the church. This distinct emphasis on church relatedness demonstrates the value of TEE in its nonformal function and orientation.

TEE programs promote individual growth in grace and spiritual maturity. Spiritual maturation is third on the list of criteria for successful programs (page 66). Accomplishing program aims correlates with the goal of developing disciples with a Pearson "r" index of association of .29 p<.02 (n=60). As an example, the president of the Alliance Church testified to the new level of Christian life brought about through those studying via ETD-Gabon.

TEE helps develop certain skills for ministry. Studying the Bible, praying, preaching, and witnessing were high on the list of skills learned (page 76). Skills are also developed as TEE students help their pastors in a wide variety of church work.

Administration

Efficient and alert administration has been discovered as a key to program success and attainment of goals. Administration includes a network of motivated people. Directors and regional coordinators keep the administrative organization tight by facilitating the outworking of discussion seminars, providing tests, grades, and certificates, and giving continual help to the tutors. They directly contribute to the overall spirit of the program, setting its tone and mood.

Research bears out the fact that programs with efficient administration and adequate staffing progress better and make greater strides toward accomplishment of their goals. Conversely the lack of an alert or qualified administration leads to weak infrastructure and eventual breakdown of the program. Turley suggests special administration courses for those who are going to lead extension programs (1991a, 50).

Some administrators mentioned lack of program structure as a cause of breakdown (page 55). Programs which expand very rapidly and then decentralize (e.g., the AIC-BEE program) tend to lose students. Bigger is not apparently better unless the program is kept at uniform quality with adequately trained leaders and centralized control.

Accurate record keeping and extrinsic rewards denote a program as official, having value and substance, especially in African cultures which appreciate formal roles. Nonformal education is not accepted as well without formal recognition. The extrinsic rewards given to students or tutors in the form of certificates, diplomas, pins, or book sacks, also tend to increase motivation.

Four out of the five case studies reveal programs which have defined courses and which give certificates and diplomas to mark the completion of those study goals. Programs with a set number of courses maintain student interest. They give the students a reasonable goal to shoot for to accomplish their purposes in development as leaders in the local church.

Variations and innovations in curriculum promote greater participant interest. These include courses from different sources (e.g., Evangelism Explosion, Child Evangelism Fellowship, SEAN, and Navigators) added to the AEAM Text-Africa series. This also provides integration between TEE and other nonformal programs. A variety of methods is being used to good advantage and offsets confusion which can often arise from the use of competing programs.

A TEE program demands that leaders concentrate on translation into the vernacular and on efficient distribution of materials. Therefore, leaders who bend over backwards to get materials to their students despite geography, lack of transport, and poor economy are to be commended. If a program cannot translate books fast enough, progress will be slowed. A lady in the ETD-Gabon program begged me to personally see to it that the AEAM Text-Africa books were translated into *all* African languages because there were so many language groups which still did not have such books.

Component Parts

Tutors, students, and administrators abundantly confirm in the case studies and questionnaires that the way component parts are handled spells the difference between a productive program and one that breaks down. We have already seen how administration, as the hub of the wheel from which the component parts operate, profoundly affects the success of the program. Now note how the component parts of TEE (students, self-study material, service, discussion, tutors, tutor training, and spiritual foundation) are interrelated in delicate balance. TEE is a flexible model and can be molded in different ways to fit different circumstances. But mishandling the component parts leads to breakdown.

The type of students which programs thrive on are well motivated, involved in serving the Lord in the local church and active in evangelism. Nothing can take the place of well motivated students. They are an essential impetus to the program. As corollary, programs with keen evangelistic and practical work emphasis develop motivation in students.

The self-study material used most advantageously is contextualized and applicable to student life. Administrators point to the contextualizing values in TEE's AEAM programmed texts. Self-study materials which are not contextualized fail to provide adequate connections for practical application and for reflection in discussion. Contextualized books facilitate this process. Where contextualization is inadequate, it all depends on the ability of the tutor to make the connection. The importance of the interdependency of the component parts is once again illustrated.

The best kind of tutors are those seasoned in church work, qualified with a broad Bible background and conversant with extension methodology. Training develops both these qualities and skills in asking questions, leading discussion, problem solving, and group dynamics.

Correlations in chapter five support the proposition that lack of tutor training contributes to breakdown in poorly led classes with little meaningful discussion (pages 83-84). Good discussion leaders are honed to perfection by regular supervision and training sessions. The low number of training sessions mentioned in chapter five contributes to less effective classes which in turn affects program development.

The discussion seminar is the heart of the praxis nature of TEE. It depends very much on the ability of the tutor to elicit discussion. The discussion in turn motivates the service component of TEE because the seminar integrates experience with the truths learned. Sharing leads to service. If the discussion fails to integrate experience and truth, learning is not as effective. Self-study material, the experience of the student and the seminar must work in harmony under an alert administration, with motivated students and trained tutors.

Together with a spiritual foundation (aims), these component parts comprise a learning force which the Holy Spirit can use to accomplish God's purposes in the world.

Problems and Causes of Breakdown

Following are the problems which focus on TEE's greatest weaknesses and probable causes of breakdown:

- Lack of funding, finances
  This is the most universal problem and is in evidence to some degree in three-quarters of the programs. Both national and missionary leaders complain about this, but national leaders put a specific emphasis on the need to fund transport.
- Lack of firm infrastructure or organization
  Infrastructure depends on capable administration. Lack of administrators rates high on the list of problems (page 73). Four out of the five case studies portrayed problems with organization, coordinators, or centralization.
- Lack of trained and qualified tutors
  Although placed midway down the list of problems, and in spite of the fact that 35% of the programs professed not to have a problem in this area, lack of trained tutors is serious. Given the pivotal position of the tutor, I believe that programs in Africa have not yet realized the critical nature and consequences of a lack of tutor training.
- Lack of church approval
  Where the church administration stands squarely behind the TEE program, greater chance of progress and continuation exist. If church or mission administrators do not understand the TEE model (or worse, downgrade it verbally), there is little encouragement for progress. Opposition may surface on the basis of offhand remarks against extension. Of the TEE programs polled, 65% reported that they "Sometimes" lacked church approval, 10% "Always" lacked church approval (page 73).

- Lack of teacher transport
  The TEE model fundamentally differs from the residence Bible school in that it depends on transport for both administrators and tutors, who travel in a circuit. The missionary usually has a vehicle and uses it in the work. The national usually does not. One of the key adjustments in turning over programs from missionaries to nationals is this matter of transport. In only one out of the three case studies where nationals head up the program did the director have transport available to him.
- Lack of books
  Sometimes books are difficult to obtain because of slow and uncertain transport. Also customs duties and inflation put books out of the financial range of the students. Sometimes not enough books have been translated to provide texts for upcoming courses.
- Difficulties in transitional times
  Programs which hand over the administrative structure to either nationals or missionaries inexperienced in TEE, unmotivated, untrained, or unsympathetic with TEE goals and methodology tend to decline. TEE depends on highly developed skills and ability to deal with complex problems over great distances. Motivated administrators are a must. Their intangible enthusiasm filters down to tutors and students. Wrongly placed leadership neutralizes the value of TEE. The length of time needed to successfully turn over a TEE program to national leadership needs careful scrutiny.

Evaluation and Future Prospects

Self-evaluation of future prospects (in the case studies) is optimistic, but does not overlook obstacles. Finances and inflation, church approval, and transition to national leadership serve to caution the programs that much careful work needs to be done to ensure a solid future.

Seventy-seven percent of TEE administrators answering Questionnaire #1 (the smaller sample) rate future prospects as good, and 67% of the larger sample (Questionnaire #2) rate prospects as good to excellent. A correlation exists between degree of fulfillment of goals with those who believe prospects are good in Questionnaire #2 (Spearman $R = .51$, $p < .00$). Clearly the great majority of programs whose goals are being fulfilled (almost 3/4 of programs) believe prospects for TEE in Africa are bright.

CHAPTER THIRTEEN

Conclusions

Success for the Christian is not "what you make it." Success involves knowing (doctrine), being (character), and doing (ministry skills) as part of accomplishing the purposes of God, or simply doing God's will. Jesus' food was to do His Father's will (John 4:34). TEE should aim for no less.

The data analysis shows that a certain level of success (as defined by criteria in chapter one) has been achieved within the range of biblically oriented goals. Although more can be done in the area of theological renewal, TEE has done much in very difficult terrain against many obstacles in Africa. The *youthfulness* of most programs should make us hesitate to judge them either quickly or harshly.

We have seen what makes TEE effective in developing leaders. Now what should churches do to guarantee the continued use, development, and prosperity of this leadership tool in the soil of Africa?

Implications

Aims

Many spiritual aims (like character development and evangelism) have been accomplished. But programs need to reexamine their aims at least every two years, and adjustments made to keep abreast of local church needs (cf. Hirst 1986). TEE programs must continually renew and refocus to keep sharp and on target.

Sponsors or stakeholders need to help administrators set goals and be sure that they (the sponsors) understand and agree to these goals. Criteria for evaluation should also be set or there will be no basis to judge whether or not aims are fulfilled. Extension that fulfills the goals set by the stakeholders makes TEE a genuine servant to the church.

Aims should be formulated regarding the type of administrators, coordinators, and tutors to be used in order to develop stronger, more permanent programs. TEE will only be as strong as the people who lead it.

Administration

The importance of administration demands that churches and missions make sure their programs build on a solid infrastructure. Specific recommendations for initiation and re-commencement are that:

1. Sponsors act decisively and diplomatically to appoint strong TEE administrators who can coordinate all segments of the program.
2. Sponsors provide administrative assistance in the form of personnel and finances.
3. Sponsors set up a TEE committee which can act as a bridge between church, mission, and TEE administrator as in the BEE case study.
4. A budget be set up for purchase of books, transport, office space, supplies, and whatever paid personnel is needed. Preplanned finances will give a sense of stability to those involved in leading the program.

TEE administration in conjunction with the sponsors must see to transportation if the "teacher-comes-to-the-student" model is to be actuated. Transportation is just as important to national leaders in carrying out the work of extension as it is to missionaries.

Widespread extension programs need to utilize intermediary supervisors or coordinators to keep in contact with tutors and classes. Large areas should be broken down to offset transportation problems. A much closer network of coordinators will be required if the infrastructure of a program is to provide the necessary help and support for tutors.

In short, sponsors of TEE programs ought to make sure that their programs are headed by knowledgable, well-motivated, and enthusiastic directors, coordinators, and tutors. "Who is doing the training?" is just as important as "what kind of training is being offered?"

I agree with the programs which refuse to start TEE classes unless the right people are in place. TEE concerns people: gifted leaders, natural leaders, and functional leaders in the local church. Without the right people, programs tend to become totally incapacitated and reduced to ineffectiveness. They also lose their reputation as a viable leadership training tool.

We should exercise much care in transition times when a change in top leadership occurs. By installing unprepared leaders, TEE will face crises which it may not survive. Overlap time must be allowed for and careful preparation made for incoming directors.

Curriculum

Extension needs a set number of courses in its curriculum, so students know where they are going and when they have finished. At the same time, TEE programs should give students more freedom in determining what they want to study, in order to meet felt needs. This is true to the adult educational principles after which TEE is modelled. It also means that TEE must develop a flexible curriculum, with electives, and be ready to use varied materials. Nationals with the gift of writing could fill the great dearth of writers.

Improvising curricular innovations at the educational level of participants, and in conjunction with them, would stimulate interest. With creativity and a willingness to try new things, TEE will continue to attract leaders who are drawn to study and want to improve their skills.

I believe programs ought to continue to give tangible awards, based on accurate record keeping, for course completion. Awards give students a sense of progress and act as a motivating factor according to the data analysis of chapter twelve (page 169).

Component Parts

The type of student must be considered carefully in devising a TEE program. Students vary greatly between those already busy in evangelism and those still trying to find their way in the church. TEE needs to focus on mature leaders as participants, or else bifurcate the program between leaders and the whole church. It would be better if specific TEE programs focused on one type only.

Some students are not ready for leadership training or gifted for leadership roles. They would best be served by a program for the whole church on a basic level of general Bible education. Leaders, on the other hand, need intensive development. Perhaps the best answer is a basic course where all start out, followed by leadership oriented courses.

Greater innovations in the area of self-study materials would foster cognitive input, including development of cassettes, instructional pictures, and videos. Of course, AEAM's contextualized and programmed books will have continued usage.

Much more effort in the translation of self-study materials into the vernacular is essential for class continuity. Committees will have to find financial sources for a series of books translated into several vernaculars if the needs of more linguistic groups are to be met. Materials on the higher level (secondary and Bible college) have to pay more attention to contextualization.

Service in the church must continue to be stressed. Most students relate to a local church, and they should be at work there. Each one should perform practical service assignments and report on them. Praxis (reflection plus action) is never complete without action, and extension students should be active. Worksheets would help students and tutors gauge service activity.

Continued evangelistic emphasis is a must because findings have shown that this is the area of greatest TEE success. More programs should develop their church planting emphasis as well.

Selection and qualification of tutors requires greater attention. Administrators should search for people gifted in maximizing class interaction. It would be better to have no class than to have a tutor unable to facilitate discussion, or one who wants to use it as a preaching opportunity. Participants should do 80% of the talking (Hall 1961, 18), not tutors.

I caution against using anyone as a tutor until he takes at least five TEE courses and carefully studies extension's training philosophy. An apprenticeship program which gradually develops potential tutors (as in ETD-Gabon) would really help a fast-growing program. No matter how great their qualifications, tutors should be provided with in-service training, including tutor manuals and workshops. As tutors receive more adequate training, discussion classes will improve. I prescribe that we carefully train tutors before initiating new classes and do not permit rapid expansion without adequately trained tutors. Unless such upgrading is instituted, the praxis element of reflection (praxis = reflection plus action) will not be employed to the best advantage.

Devote more time to discussion in seminars, and less to the formalities of taking attendance and grading quizzes. Just as tutors require briefing on how to conduct classes, so should students be briefed on what is expected of them. This would also facilitate discussion and maximize student potential.

If we can develop problem solving among students in the discussion seminar to a greater degree, we will be giving them a vital tool for the Christian life. If the class ignores real life problems, it will shortly become irrelevant. Participants cannot grow as leaders without the ability to solve problems, while those who can solve problems will be regarded as the true leaders.

External Relationships

Before a TEE program is begun, full local and denominational approval should be obtained. If necessary, begin a pilot program to demonstrate the model to the church. The extra time will be worth it.

An extension program begun without full church approval should attempt in every way to secure the blessing of the church and maintain a good relationship with it. By taking two steps backward we may be able to go forward on more solid ground. Those with such approval should seek at all times to deepen their relationship to the church. Integration with the local church adds to TEE's effectiveness as students have the right context in which to serve the Lord. TEE cannot exist in isolation from the church.

Denominations and missions which endorse TEE programs need to demonstrate that their approval as sponsors is not out of politeness, but is genuine. It takes time for a program to prove its benefit to the church. Once the church approves TEE, it should not neglect its responsibility to it but act as a true facilitator.

TEE programs must maintain a broad publicity throughout all the churches it serves, so that all know what extension is and does as a servant to the church. The time taken to create an atmosphere for church-based leadership formation will help participants have the right expectations.

Relationships with academic institutions for accreditation is important. Many extension schools seek accreditation. The function of leadership development, however, should not be dependent on accreditation and should continue whether or not they obtain it. The demands for developing leaders are very compelling and cannot wait for academia.

Recommendations for Further Study

This study has not only been descriptive but has sought to lay a basis to answer an evaluative question, "What makes TEE effective?" Further experimental and evaluative research should be carried out on TEE in Africa and other continents. More descriptive case studies ought to be written in an attempt to get an accurate picture of TEE. Self evaluation is necessary for administrators of churches to determine if they are getting a good return on their investment, the wisest use of their funds for leadership development.

Experimental studies will have to be conducted to see the precise effects of tutor training on discussion seminar performance. Effective performance can only be tested by examining results of an experimental group (with additional training classes) and a control group (without any special training classes).

Group dynamic studies using sociograms to determine the extent and quality of group interaction would be valuable. Particular classes could be plotted and the extent of interaction measured over a term or a year.

A study on the effect of cultural forms of education on the TEE model would be relevant. Sitting in a circle in a learning situation is so natural for Africans in view of their traditional way of eating, talking, and solving problems. What other factors in African cultural education are conducive to TEE? What factors (such as reading and lectures) from the imposition of European culture make it difficult for TEE to prosper, and why? Lectures are diametrically opposed to the discussion techniques used in TEE.

A wide vista of research on extension accreditation is opening up. Ferris has set standards that demand consideration. Accreditation in relation to residence schools will be tackled by ACTEA, but it may take years to determine standards acceptable to both forms of training.

I recommend that evaluative studies be conducted in particular areas—East Africa, Central Africa, West Africa, and Southern Africa. Programs could be compared and evaluated to find out what is working, and if they are accomplishing their goals. By sharing knowledge *within their area*, programs with similar conditions could improve their performance.

Research is needed on the funding of TEE programs. What percentage do the students' fees provide? What new price increases should be made to improve programs. What are the sources of grants? Are there other ways to finance TEE programs? How does the payment of student fees correlate with the overall health of a program?

Recognizing the difficulties of transition times when an experienced leader is replaced, a detailed methodology for the preparation of extension administrators needs to be developed. Sponsoring bodies which take seriously the qualifications for appointment of a TEE director should devise an administrative manual to provide some basic training for the job.

More studies are necessary to describe, test, and evaluate the effectiveness of TEE as a leadership development tool. Researchers interested and committed to leadership development in Africa are needed to do such work.

Concluding Challenge

Above all, TEE has to reassert itself as a catalyst for continued evangelism, development of pastoral skills, and character in the praxis model of theological education.

Pulse reports that over 21,000 people are being trained through TEE in Africa (1991, 1). Many more leaders can be developed as TEE gives believers a forum for contextualizing the Word of God in their situation.

I call TEE leadership to work with new determination and persistence for the renewal of God's purposes for the local church.

Urbanization & TEE in Kenya Questionnaire

Cross Tabulation by Urban/Rural Location
Interim Draft Report
10 November 1990

(Prepared by the Urban Ministries Support Group with assistance from Mrs. Marsha Navamanie, Daystar University College, and Rev. Phillip Turley, AIC-BEE)

Over 200 questionnaires were sent out to selected TEE students in Kenya. To date 98 have been returned and included in this preliminary analysis. One of the purposes of the study was to see whether TEE students living in urban areas differed significantly from those living in rural areas. Of the 98 students who completed questionnaires 48 were classified as urban and 50 were classified as rural. The respondents were primarily from four programmes: AGC, AIC, ICM, and KAG.

How many TEE courses had been taken? Urbanites seem to predominate on the low end of the scale while rural dwellers do so on the other end. The high mobility of urban dwellers may be a factor here. Both groups spend a similar amount of time in course preparation.

Language preferences are as would be expected with English being more likely the reading preference of urbanites and mother tongue the preference of rural people. Swahili is used about equally.

There was an interesting difference in responses to the question why they were taking the TEE course (see attached results summary) but the difference is not likely to be significant for our purposes.

Rural people are likely to make more money available for TEE courses than urbanites. Possibly because of fewer competing demands for cash and fewer educational alternatives.

The statements from "The material in my course is easy to read/ understand" through "Transportation to TEE classes is difficult for me" show an amazing similarity of response. One might well expect that urbanites would express more schedule-oriented conflicts than rural dwellers. One slight difference that shows up is in increased responsibility in church as a result of TEE studies with rural people having more response from their churches than city dwellers. Might this be because urban churches think less highly of TEE and that urban students are a bit younger? Also, it seems that urban people are slightly more likely to have trouble getting to class than rural people.

Urban students are predominantly male in contrast to rural students who are about equally divided between male and female.

The following tables have been simplified by removing some figures such as the number of missing responses. So in some cases the reported totals do not match the numbers shown.

The numbers are actual numbers of responses. Because the total responses are close to 100, the numbers are also close to the percentages of the total.

Not all of the differences in categories of response are statistically significant.

	1 Urban	2 Rural	N %

Column 1

**Program of questionnaire respondents

	Urban	Rural	N %
PAG-TEE	2	0	2
Baptist TEE	0	0	0
AGC-TEE	0	26	26
AIC-BEE	21	16	37
ICM-TEE	15	0	15
KAG-TEE	10	8	18
N	48	50	98

Column 3

***How many TEE courses have you studied?

	Urban	Rural	N %
1	14	7	21
2 to 3	16	11	27
3 to 5	9	5	14
6 to 8	5	3	8
9 to 11	0	2	2
12 or more	1	22	23
N	48	50	98

Column 4

**How much time do you spend each week preparing?

less than 2 hours	12	8	20
2 to 3 hours	12	13	25
4 to 7 hours	11	17	28
more than 7 hours	10	5	15
N	48	50	98

Column 5

**Which language do you prefer to read?

English	29	16	45
Swahili	17	13	30
Mother tongue	1	18	19
Other	0	0	0
N	48	50	98

Column 6

**Which language do you prefer to speak at home?

English	2	0	2
Swahili	12	7	19
Mother tongue	34	42	76
Other	0	0	0
N	48	50	98

Column 7

**Which language is used in your TEE class?

English	21	2	23
Swahili	26	21	47
Mother tongue	0	25	25
Other	0	0	0
N	48	50	98

Column 8

Which languages do you read well? - English

Yes	42	27	69

Column 9

Which languages do you read well? - Swahili

Yes	32	30	62

Column 10

Which languages do you read well? - Mother

Yes	27	43	70

Column 11

Which languages to you read well? - Other

Yes	2	1	3

Column 12

Which languages do you speak well? - English

Yes	38	20	58

Column 13

Which languages do you speak well? - Swahili

Yes	6	25	41

Column 14

Which languages do you speak well? - Mother

Yes	36	43	79

Column 15

**Which language do you speak well? - Other

Yes	2	1	3

Column 16

**Why are you taking the TEE course?

Upgrade my Bible knowledge	14	10	24
Be a better Christian	31	31	44
Serve better in my church	21	7	28
Become a pastor	0	1	1
Other	0	0	0
N	48	50	98

Column 17

**How often would you like to meet as a class?

One time per week	26	31	57
Two times per week	15	16	31
One time per month	0	1	1
Two times per month	0	0	0
N	48	50	98

Column 18

**Would you prefer to do all of your study...

In the class together	9	19	28
At home alone	1	0	1
Prepare at home & meet together	38	31	69
N	48	50	98

Column 19

**What is the most you can pay for a TEE course?

Less than Ksh 60	28	12	40
Ksh 60 to 100	17	27	44
Ksh 101 to 150	1	9	10
More than Ksh 150	1	2	3
N	48	50	98

Column 20

**The material in my course is easy to read/understand.

Agree	45	45	90
Neither agree nor disagree	2	2	4
Disagree	1	3	4
N	48	50	98

Column 21

**I like classes that meet in someone's home.

Agree	4	10	14
Neither agree nor disagree	11	9	20
Disagree	31	28	59
N	48	50	98

Column 22

**The class time is boring.

Agree	2	2	4
Neither agree not disagree	5	5	10
Disagree	39	41	80
N	48	50	98

Column 23

**The things I learn in class I am able to use.

Agree	41	43	84
Neither agree nor disagree	2	2	4
Disagree	2	2	4
N	48	50	98

Column 24

**I learn more when the teacher lectures.

Agree	5	6	11
Neither agree nor disagree	4	9	13
Disagree	39	33	72
N	48	50	98

Column 25

**I would like classes to be held in a real school room.

Agree	20	25	45
Neither agree nor disagree	11	7	18
Disagree	16	18	34
N	48	50	98

Column 26

**My study has helped me lead someone to the Lord.

Agree	42	45	87
Neither agree nor disagree	4	1	5
Disagree	2	4	6
N	48	50	98

Column 27

**TEE classes require more time for study than available.

Agree	28	24	52
Neither agree nor disagree	4	6	10
Disagree	16	20	36
N	48	50	98

Column 28

**I have been given church work because of TEE.

Agree	16	23	39
Neither agree nor disagree	7	12	19
Disagree	25	13	38
N	48	50	98

Column 29

**My family responsibilities interfere with TEE classes.

Agree	12	12	24
Neither agree nor disagree	6	3	9
Disagree	25	39	64
N	48	50	98

Column 30

**The TEE book we use has information I need to know.

Agree	43	41	84
Neither agree nor disagree	4	4	8
Disagree	1	3	4
N	48	50	98

Column 31

**Studying TEE has improved my family life.

Agree	44	50	98
Neither agree nor disagree	4	0	4
Disagree	0	0	0
N	48	50	98

Column 32

**My pastor is glad that I study TEE.

Agree	41	45	86
Neither agree nor disagree	6	3	9
Disagree	1	1	2
N	48	50	98

Column 33

**Studying TEE helps me get along better with workmates.

Agree	41	41	82
Neither agree nor disagree	4	5	9
Disagree	3	2	5
N	48	50	98

Column 34

**TEE class time fits my personal schedule.

Agree	34	39	73
Neither agree nor disagree	6	7	13
Disagree	8	3	11
N	48	50	98

Column 35

**My work makes it difficult to attend TEE courses.

Agree	13	8	21
Neither agree nor disagree	2	4	6
Disagree	33	38	71
N	48	50	98

Column 36

**Transportation to TEE classes is difficult for me.

Agree	9	2	11
Neither agree nor disagree	5	2	7
Disagree	33	46	79
N	48	50	98

Column 37

**How old are you?

Under 20	0	3	3
21 - 30	19	9	28
31 - 40	17	24	41
41 - 50	10	13	23
Over 50	2	1	3
N	48	50	98

Column 38

**What is your sex?

Male	39	24	63
Female	9	22	31
N	48	49	97

Column 39

**What is your marital status?

Single	11	7	18
Married	37	40	77
Divorced/Separated	0	0	0
Widowed	0	0	0
N	48	50	98

Column 40

**How much schooling have you completed before TEE?

None	0	2	2
Primary	5	22	27
Secondary	28	13	41
Technical School	3	4	7
College/Diploma	12	9	21
University or higher	0	0	0
N	48	50	98

Column 41

**Which of the following describes your work?

Unemployed	3	2	5
Student	4	2	6
Full-time pastor/church worker	4	6	10
Professional	6	5	11
Salaried Worker	21	14	35
Business Person	4	0	4
Farmer	1	8	9
Management/Administration	3	1	4
Housewife	2	12	14
Other	0	0	0
N	48	50	98

Column 42

**What is your current position in your church?

Pastor	2	8	10
Elder/Deacon	27	7	34
Lay Reader	1	10	11
Sunday School Teacher	4	7	11
Evangelist	3	8	11
Other	0	0	0
N	48	50	98

ACTEA All-Africa Conference of Theological Educators

---

30 May to 3 June 1990
Limuru, Kenya

TEE Workshop

A. David Kornfield's list of TEE weaknesses: Reproduced from *Cyprus: TEE Come of Age*, ed. Robert L. Youngblood, Great Britain: The Paternoster Press, no date, pp. 17, 18.

1. The failure of students to complete assignments because of involvement in more pressing matters.

2. Lack of identification of the educator with his students. Because of the brevity of the time spent in each extension center a growing personal relationship is difficult to establish.

3. Lack of time for the educator to be with his family since he is constantly traveling from center to center.

4. Lack of being able to graduate in a relatively short period of time since to cover the same number of courses as a residential seminary would require between two and three times as many years.

5. Too much hinges on one individual teacher and there is lack of exposure to many teachers with varying fields, abilities and vision.

6. It is too easy to quit since there is little initial sacrifice involved in becoming part of the program.

7. The traveling itinerary could be quite expensive.

8. It would be difficult to be involved in evaluation of nonwritten assignments and of practical applications of the learner's studies.

9. The role of the educator, even more than in the residential setting, perhaps, would be that of providing cognitive input in a limited amount of time, so that affective and behavioral changes would have to occur at the students' initiative.

10. The lack of resources in many cases, both written and human, to turn to for help during the interim period between the extension educator's visits.

B. Responses and solutions to Kornfield's list of TEE weaknesses provided by various TEE programme leaders in Africa.

1. *Failure of students to complete assignments:*
   a. Three ideas by Hodgins of TEEM in Malawi: First, keep assignments brief. Use multiple choice and short answers rather than essays. Secondly, circulate among students and remind them of assignments coming due. Thirdly, TEEM pays those tutors who mark assignments by the number of assignments they mark. Thus the tutors pay more attention to encouraging students to complete their work.
   b. Two ideas by Fehr of ETD in Gabon: First, ETD includes assignments as a part of the student's grade. Secondly, reports on the assignments are allowed to be given orally instead of always requiring a written report.
   c. Two ideas by Gaddis of TEE in Zimbabwe: Unfinished lessons at the time of a class resulted in a reduction in score for that class quiz. And at the end of the course, the lessons must be fully completed to receive credit for the course.
   d. Muraran of AGC-TEE in Kenya stressed that prospective students should be made fully aware of the course requirements including the assignments prior to enrolling them.

2. *Lack of identification of the educator with his students:*
   a. Hodgins of TEEM in Malawi suggests: If you have a small staff covering a large area, focus activity on certain geographical areas for perhaps the duration of a course series

(in our case 2 years). Then move from area to area providing each with the substantive student-teacher contact needed.

   b. Two ideas by Fehr of ETD in Gabon: First, they provide trimestrial retreats and out-of-class activities. Secondly, they are using former students to become teachers within their own local area which maximizes the student-teacher contact.

   c. Two ideas from Gaddis of TEE in Zimbabwe: They use biannual retreats to bring teachers and students together and also require a student interview annually to assess progress.

   d. Muraran of AGC-TEE in Kenya says: For those programmes where the teacher meets with the students once a week for discussion classes, this should not be a problem.

3. *Lack of time for the educator to be with his family:*

   a. Hodgins of TEEM in Malawi: See his suggestion for number 2 above, letter "a". He cautions that we should not put cost effectiveness above other considerations, such as the quality of family life for teachers.

   b. Muraran of AGC-TEE in Kenya says 3 things: The teacher should have good means of transportation. He should not be given too many classes. And they make sure all of their teachers get one full working day off per week.

4. *Unable to graduate in a relatively short period of time:*

   a. Hodgins of TEEM in Malawi: The programme is a 2 year series, hence the problem does not exist for them.

   b. Fehr of ETD in Gabon: First, they have tried to develop long term study as an asset. They emphasize that continuing education while you serve is a norm. Secondly, they have an institute which allows students to take 2 or 3 classes at night which allows them to complete a course of study more rapidly.

5. *Too much hinges on one individual teacher:*

   a. Fehr of ETD in Gabon says: Holding seminars and condensed courses where a teacher who is specialized in a particular area helps to offset the single teacher problem.

   b. Gaddis of TEE in Zimbabwe: First, the programmed text as the teacher resolves this problem since the books are

by a variety of teachers. In addition, the class leaders could
be rotated so that they take different classes.

c. Turley of AIC-BEE in Kenya: We are turning our resources
to the attention of developing our teachers so they can make
more significant contributions. We are improving the
teacher training course, providing an annual teacher conference which is both instructional and motivational, regional teacher meetings for the same purpose, and teacher
awards for service which consist of a certificate and a
resource book such as a commentary or Bible dictionary.
We are also preparing teachers' guidebooks to provide
helpful information and suggested discussion questions.
Finally, we are trying to build a scholarship fund to provide
long term teachers with help to upgrade their own abilities.

6   *It is too easy to quit as there is little initial sacrifice:*
a. Hodgins of TEEM in Malawi: The issue isn't sacrifice, but
selectivity. We should know the prospective students and
select them carefully.
b. Muraran of AGC-TEE in Kenya: There are several levels
within the programme besides the final graduation. People
who only make it to level 1 or 2 are still eligible to be used
in ministry.

7. *Travel is expensive:*
Hodgins of TEEM in Malawi: Motorbikes are inexpensive and
avoid the problem of an elitist impression given by driving a
car.

8. *Difficulty of evaluation of nonwritten and practical assignments:*
a. Snook of TEE-TEAM in South Africa suggests 7 things:
1) Student discussion should reflect what they apply in
ministry.
2) Oral reports can be given in class.
3) Students can turn in written reports of their work.
4) Pastor-supervisors can give written reports about the
student.
5) Teachers can sometimes observe student ministries.
6) Students from a single church could do a joint project to
plot the effect of their work on church growth.
7) The final test score should reflect the evaluation of
practical assignments.

b. Hodgins of TEEM in Malawi: This is more easily done by the teacher if you follow the concept in number 2, letter "a".

c. Fehr of ETD in Gabon: First, the student can do a self-evaluation. Secondly, he can turn in a weekly written report of his work.

9. *Inadequate time for the teacher to impact affective and behavioral changes in the student:*
Everyone disagreed with this point by Kornfield. They felt that since the teaching material had presented the cognitive input, then the TEE teacher, even more than the residential teacher, has time to discuss application and behavioral changes. Gaddis of TEE in Zimbabwe added that they also have prepared teacher's guides which suggest many affective type activities to promote change in the student.

10. *Lack of human and written resources to help students between classes.*
a. Hodgins of TEEM in Malawi: We provide a library service by post. Also, we are doing limited publication of additional resource materials.

b. Pierce of PEDIM in Burkino Faso mentions 5 things: First, they produce their own materials and include in it extra resource material such as what might be found in a Bible dictionary, commentary, etc. Secondly, they provide leaders' manuals with additional material. Thirdly, they provide periodic teaching sessions for their leaders. Fourthly, their educators are local pastors or missionaries and so are nearby and available to help. Finally, they are establishing a small library to provide for each center.

C. Recommendations to help African TEE programmes made to the ACTEA Commission for TEE at a consultation held in Kenya in 1987. These will form the basis of discussion for the last workshop in our series.

1. Advise as to standards for a well-rounded TEE program.

2. Accredit materials, critique those available, and begin writing of additional materials.

3. Standardize terminology or provide equivalence of terms.

4. Recommend equivalence lengths for courses in relation to residential programs.

5. Credibility in village (lower) levels.

6. Start with diploma levels and then spread to other higher and lower.

7. Formulate Public Relations materials and marketing methods for programs.

8. Watch for gaps in the continental program.

9. Undertake and support research projects and surveys.

10. Act as clearing house for information and research.

11. Determine who we are reaching and how many.

12. Development of forms, consultant for surveys, and regional coordination.

13. How-To-Do TEE kit with a compendium of pitfalls to avoid, etc.

14. Publicize AC-TEE formation, encourage forming of associations, regional networking, etc.

15. Form a publications sub-committee.

16. Identify needs and encourage course development across the continent.

17. Develop TEE tools and studies with listing of programs.

18. Develop a directory of personnel, administrators, writers and consultants.

19. Provide information for library development and act as clearing house for curriculum.

20. Provide guidelines or recommendations of how to transfer from expatriate to national leadership.

21. Monograph series: TEE and the Church, Residential Program and Finance.

22. Need guidelines and purpose for organizations, terms of reference.

23. Bulletin for linkage, innovation, workshops, conferences, lectures, new publications, reviews, etc.

Questionnaire #1

An open-ended questionnaire distributed to
selected TEE administrators at the
All Africa Theological Educators Conference
Limuru, Kenya—June 1990

1. Would you classify your TEE program a success?

   Yes _____   No _____

2. If a success, what signals to you that it is a success? If not a success, why not?

   _____

   _____

   _____

3. If your program is failing or has broken down, to what do you attribute this failure or breakdown? (If several reasons, please list.)

   _____

   _____

   _____

4. How many workers have been trained (i.e., graduated) over the past three years? _____ The past ten years? _____

5. How many are laymen? _____ How many are pastors? _____

6. How many TEE students have led others to Christ? _____
   (Please estimate if you do not have exact figures.)

   Have these students brought others into their local churches? _____
   (Please estimate the numbers if you do not have the exact figures.)

   Indicate the time: in 1 year; in 2 years; in 5 years; etc.

   If not, could you give some figures regarding the number of people who have attended over a three to five year period:

   Church 1: from _____ to _____

   Church 2: from _____ to _____

   Church 3: from _____ to _____

   Church 4: from _____ to _____

   Church 5: from _____ to _____

7. What kind of self-study books does your training program use?

   _____

   _____

   _____

8. What are some of the common problems in running your TEE program?

   (1) _____

   (2) _____

   (3) _____

   (4) _____

   (5) _____

9. Which problems have caused total breakdown?

    _____

    _____

10. Is your TEE program connected with an evangelism program in your
    local church? Yes _____   No _____

    Please explain: _____

    _____

11. How do you view the future prospects of TEE?

         Good _____   Bad _____   Indifferent _____

12. Is your program meeting the needs of educated Africans?

         Yes _____   No _____

    Other Comment: _____

    _____

13. How many matriculants are in your program? _____

14. Would educated Africans in your area like a different kind of self-study
    book?   Yes _____   No _____

    Explain: _____

    _____

15. Do you have problems with equivalency with residence training?

    Yes _____ No _____

16. What are some of these problems: _____

_____

_____

17. Does TEE relate at all to social/health needs of your area?

Yes _____ No _____

18. If yes, how has TEE affected the community healthwise, politically, so-
cially or economically?

_____

_____

_____

19. What skills are your program teaching?

_____

_____

_____

20. Can you give a brief sketch of one or two leaders who have benefitted
from your TEE program? Please describe how each was helped. Use extra
paper if necessary.

_____

_____

_____

_____

_____

_____

21. In what ways has TEE lessened the load of pastors of your area in the work of preaching, visiting and witnessing?

_____

_____

_____

_____

How many years does the average student in your program study?

_____ (years)

22. Does your TEE program have all the component parts of TEE? (Spiritual base, self-study books, discussion classes, service in the local church.)

Yes _____ No _____

If not, what does it lack?

_____

_____

23. Is your TEE program geared to lay training, pastoral training, or both?

_____

24. Has TEE aided in contextualizing the Gospel—that is, do more people in the community understand the Gospel because you have a TEE program?

Yes _____   No _____

How do you know?

_____

_____

_____

_____

25. Please give the correct name and address of your school here:

Name: _____

Address: _____

_____

_____

26. Total number of students: _____

27. Please list the number of students in each class:

Class 1 _____   Class 4 _____

Class 2 _____   Class 5 _____

Class 3 _____   Class 6 _____

If you have more than six classes, please use the bottom half of the paper to list them.

28. Number of monitors (discussion group leaders): _____

Any additional information you wish to add here will be welcomed. Please note especially any difference or variations from a regular TEE structure.

Questionnaire #2

A closed questionnaire distributed to administrators
of all TEE programs in Africa
December 1990

Your name: _____

Your position: _____

Name of your TEE program: _____

Address of program: _____

_____

Phone number: _____ Fax _____
(Please include country and/or area code)

Please check the answer which is best in your context from an administrators point of view and knowledge.

This first section deals with the background of your program.

1. How long has your extension program been in operation? **Check one.**

    01. 0–3 years .... [ ]
    02. 4–6 years .... [ ]
    03. 7–10 years .... [ ]
    04. 11–13 years .... [ ]
    05. 14–17 years .... [ ]
    06. 18–20 years .... [ ]
    07. above 21 years .... [ ]

2. What was the original and primary aim of your TEE program? **Check** the appropriate squares.

	No	Somewhat	Yes
01. Teach Bible content	[ ]	[ ]	[ ]
02. Train in pastoral skills	[ ]	[ ]	[ ]
03. Train for lay leadership	[ ]	[ ]	[ ]
04. Develop disciples	[ ]	[ ]	[ ]
05. Develop Christian character	[ ]	[ ]	[ ]
06. Other (specify): _____	[ ]	[ ]	[ ]

3. What was the target group for your TEE program? Check **Yes** or **No.**

	Yes	No
01. All Christians	[ ]	[ ]
02. Only Local Church Leaders	[ ]	[ ]
03. Only Pastors	[ ]	[ ]
04. Both Pastors and Lay Leaders	[ ]	[ ]
05. Everyone	[ ]	[ ]

4. What criteria of success or effectiveness would you use for your program? **Check one** which indicates degree of importance:

Students . . .

	Very	Somewhat	Not at all
01. attend regularly	[ ]	[ ]	[ ]
02. complete workbooks	[ ]	[ ]	[ ]
03. witness to others	[ ]	[ ]	[ ]
04. work in local church	[ ]	[ ]	[ ]
05. help their pastor	[ ]	[ ]	[ ]
06. solve problems	[ ]	[ ]	[ ]
07. mature spiritually	[ ]	[ ]	[ ]

5. Do you feel that you have accomplished the original aim of your TEE program? **Check one** which indicates the degree to which you feel it is accomplished.

01. Not at all fulfilled	[ ]
02. Somewhat fulfilled	[ ]
03. Uncertain	[ ]
04. Is being fulfilled	[ ]
05. Greatly fulfilled	[ ]

Please list other aim(s) which have been fulfilled:

01. _____

02. _____

Please list other aim(s) which have not been fulfilled:

01. _____

02. _____

6. What kind of self-study books or materials does your program use? If you do not use books indicate other kind of material.

01. AEAM programmed texts .... [ ]
02. SEAN .... [ ]
03. Cassettes .... [ ]
04. Your own texts .... [ ]
05. Your own and AEAM texts .... [ ]
06. Regular text books .... [ ]
07. Other _____ [ ]

7. Where do your students do their practical work or service for the Lord?

01. In an established church .... [ ]
02. With a parachurch group .... [ ]
03. In a new church planting situation .... [ ]
04. Community development .... [ ]
05. Other _____ [ ]

The following questions have to do with TEE and church growth.

8. Do you see evidence that your TEE students are helping their local churches to grow? **Check one.**

01. Yes, they are .... [ ]
02. Uncertain .... [ ]
03. Sometimes .... [ ]
04. No, they are not .... [ ]

9. In what way are your TEE students helping their churches to grow?
   Check how often you see these things:

	Never	Seldom	Sometimes	Always
01. They bring new people	[ ]	[ ]	[ ]	[ ]
02. They witness to others	[ ]	[ ]	[ ]	[ ]
03. They help others	[ ]	[ ]	[ ]	[ ]
04. They lead services	[ ]	[ ]	[ ]	[ ]
05. They stop fights	[ ]	[ ]	[ ]	[ ]
06. They preach/teach Bible ...	[ ]	[ ]	[ ]	[ ]
07. Other _____	[ ]	[ ]	[ ]	[ ]

The following questions have to do with problems/difficulties.

10. What things are causing problems in your program? **Check** the most
    appropriate box next to the problem.

	Never	Sometimes	Always
01. Lack of books/material	[ ]	[ ]	[ ]
02. Lack of competent administrators	[ ]	[ ]	[ ]
03. Untrained seminar leaders	[ ]	[ ]	[ ]
04. Lack of church support	[ ]	[ ]	[ ]
05. Poorly motivated students.................	[ ]	[ ]	[ ]
06. Inability to do workbooks	[ ]	[ ]	[ ]
07. Lack of teacher transport	[ ]	[ ]	[ ]
08. Lack of funding	[ ]	[ ]	[ ]
09. Failure to pay student fees.................	[ ]	[ ]	[ ]
10. Lack of place to meet	[ ]	[ ]	[ ]
11. Failure to keep attendance	[ ]	[ ]	[ ]
12. Other _____	[ ]	[ ]	[ ]

The following questions have to do with the kind of skills your training
offers.

11. How are your students in your program linked with an evangelistic
    program in your local church? **Check** the appropriate boxes:

	Always	Sometimes	Seldom	Not Sure
01. They evangelize on their own	[ ]	[ ]	[ ]	[ ]
02. They evangelize with their pastor	[ ]	[ ]	[ ]	[ ]
03. They evangelize in teams..............	[ ]	[ ]	[ ]	[ ]
04. Other _____	[ ]	[ ]	[ ]	[ ]

12. For Church related programs what skills are your students developing through your TEE program? **Check** the appropriate box.

	None	Some	Many
01. Witnessing	[ ]	[ ]	[ ]
02. Counselling	[ ]	[ ]	[ ]
03. Preaching	[ ]	[ ]	[ ]
04. Leading Bible study	[ ]	[ ]	[ ]
05. Studying the Bible	[ ]	[ ]	[ ]
06. Leading worship	[ ]	[ ]	[ ]
07. Praying	[ ]	[ ]	[ ]
08. Other _____	[ ]	[ ]	[ ]

13. What community related skills are being developed as a result of your TEE program?

	None	Some	Many
01. Health Care	[ ]	[ ]	[ ]
02. Political skill	[ ]	[ ]	[ ]
03. Farming ability	[ ]	[ ]	[ ]
04. Legal ability	[ ]	[ ]	[ ]
05. Finding work	[ ]	[ ]	[ ]

14. How do students help their pastor outside of class? **Check** only what you know they do.

	Never	Sometimes	Always
01. Visit members with him	[ ]	[ ]	[ ]
02. Lead worship services	[ ]	[ ]	[ ]
03. Visit the sick	[ ]	[ ]	[ ]
04. Bring others to church	[ ]	[ ]	[ ]
05. Witness to the unsaved	[ ]	[ ]	[ ]
06. Counsel with sorrowing	[ ]	[ ]	[ ]
07. Other _____	[ ]	[ ]	[ ]

The next few questions have to do with the discussion class and discussion group leader (monitor).

15. What do <u>others</u> report about your discussion group leaders when they lead their classes?

	Never	Sometimes	Always
01. They do most of the talking	[ ]	[ ]	[ ]
02. They get others to talk	[ ]	[ ]	[ ]
03. They repeat the day's lesson	[ ]	[ ]	[ ]
04. They help solve problems	[ ]	[ ]	[ ]
05. They give quizzes	[ ]	[ ]	[ ]
06. They review at end of class	[ ]	[ ]	[ ]
07. They begin with prayer	[ ]	[ ]	[ ]
08. Other _____	[ ]	[ ]	[ ]

16. Do your discussion group leaders (monitors/tutors) report that they are doing problem solving in the class?
Check one.

01. Yes .... [ ]
02. Uncertain .... [ ]
03. No .... [ ]

17. Do your discussion group leaders report that there is good interaction between the students. **Choose what is usually reported.**

01 Yes .... [ ]
02. No .... [ ]
03. Uncertain .... [ ]

18. What kind of discussion group leaders (monitors) are used in your program? **Check the appropriate boxes.**

	Never	Sometimes	Often
01. Former TEE students with no Bible school	[ ]	[ ]	[ ]
02. Pastors with no TEE experience	[ ]	[ ]	[ ]
03. Pastors with TEE experience	[ ]	[ ]	[ ]
04. Bible school graduates with TEE experience	[ ]	[ ]	[ ]
05. Bible school graduates with no TEE experience	[ ]	[ ]	[ ]
06. Other _____	[ ]	[ ]	[ ]

19. What kind of training does your TEE program provide for the TEE discussion group leaders (monitors)?

	Never	Sometimes	Often
01. We give the basic training .... [ ]		[ ]	[ ]
02. We improve their questioning abilities .... [ ]		[ ]	[ ]
03. We show them how to keep student interaction going .... [ ]		[ ]	[ ]
04. We show them how to help students solve problems .... [ ]		[ ]	[ ]
05. Other _____ [ ]		[ ]	[ ]

20. How many training sessions have you held for your discussion group leaders ...

01. This calendar year .... [ ]
02. Last calendar year .... [ ]

These questions are evaluative in nature and ask your opinion on your program in general.

21. The experience of people studying through TEE classes is helping them to learn to think. How strongly do you agree or disagree with this statement? **Check** the most appropriate box.

01. Strongly Disagree .... [ ]
02. More or Less Agree ...... [ ]
03. Strongly Agree.............. [ ]

22. Recognizing that changes may be needed, what do you need the most to make your TEE classes better? Choose either one OR check all that apply.

01. books .... [ ]
02. discussion leaders .... [ ]
03. students .... [ ]
04. methods .... [ ]
05. places to meet .... [ ]
06. other _____ [ ]

23. If you could select better self-study material, what would you like to see in them? Books with more . . .

	Yes	No	Uncertain
01. pictures	[ ]	[ ]	[ ]
02. reading	[ ]	[ ]	[ ]
03. diagrams	[ ]	[ ]	[ ]
04. discussion questions	[ ]	[ ]	[ ]
05. project ideas	[ ]	[ ]	[ ]
06. other _____	[ ]	[ ]	[ ]

24. What are the future prospects of TEE in your situation? **Check one** that seems most accurate.

01. Poor .... [ ]
02. Fair .... [ ]
03. Good .... [ ]
04. Excellent .... [ ]

25. Do you think that the original aims of your TEE program are being fulfilled? **Choose one.**

01. No, it is not .... [ ]
02. Yes, somewhat .... [ ]
03. Yes, it is .... [ ]
04. Very much so .... [ ]

The last questions deal with whether your program is formal or nonformal in nature.

26. Please indicate the kind of relationship you have with an academic institution.

01. None .... [ ]
02. Loosely linked with one... [ ]
03. Parallel with one .... [ ]
04. Part of it .... [ ]

27. Please indicate if you are accredited from an academic institution. (That is, you receive grades and certification through such an institution.)

    01. Yes .... [ ]
    02. No .... [ ]
    03. Other .... [ ] _____

28. Please indicate if you are a nonformal program, i.e., you do not give grades to your students.

	Yes	No
01. We give grades	[ ]	[ ]
02. We give certificates	[ ]	[ ]
03. We have certain days of recognition	[ ]	[ ]
04. The church recognizes those who study	[ ]	[ ]
05. Other _____	[ ]	[ ]

29. Please indicate if you train local church leaders only.

    01. Yes .... [ ]
    02. No .... [ ]

Thank you for taking the time to fill out this questionnaire. I believe this information will be helpful to my research. If you wish a copy of the results of this questionnaire, please write to:

The Billy Graham Center
Wheaton College
Wheaton, IL 60187
U.S.A.

Bibliography

ACTEA. 1990. TEE weaknesses. A paper prepared for the TEE track. 30 May to 3 June. Limuru, Kenya: All Africa Theological Educators Conference.

Anderson, Keith B. and N. Kiranga Gatimu. 1983. Diocese of Mt. Kenya East (Anglican): Meeting community needs through theological education by extension. In *Ministry by the people: Theological education by extension.* Ed. F. Ross Kinsler. Maryknoll, NY: Orbis Books.

Apps, Jerold W. 1979. *Problems in continuing education.* New York, NY: McGraw-Hill Book Company.

Baird, John E. Jr. and Sanford B. Weinberg. 1981. *Group communication: The essence of synergy.* Dubuque, IA: Wm. C. Brown Company Publishers.

Baker, George A. III. 1983. Serving undereducated adults: Community as learning center. In *Educational outreach to select adult populations.* Ed. Carol E. Kasworm. *New directions for continuing education.* San Francisco, CA: Jossey Bass Publishers. 20 (December): 31-42.

Baker, Milton G. 1969. Taking theological education to the students. In *Theological education by extension.* Ed. Ralph D. Winter. Pasadena, CA: William Carey Library.

Barnett, Ted. 1991. Theological education: Another look. *AIM International.* 75.1 (Winter): 1, 4-5.

Bates, Gerald. 1971. A report on the first CAMEO workshops in Africa. October. Wheaton College, Wheaton, IL: Billy Graham Center Archives.

Bi-annual Report. 1991. An unpublished report to the African Inland Church by the national BEE coordinator. April. Nairobi, Kenya.

Bray, Mark. 1984. Obstacles to nonformal education development: The case of Papua, New Guinea. *Convergence*. 17.2: 43-50.

Brief history of COCIN-EBS. 1990. An unpublished summary of the beginnings and curriculum offered. Jos, Nigeria.

Brookfield, Stephen D. 1987. *Understanding and facilitating adult learning*. San Francisco, CA: Jossey-Bass Publishers.

Bruner, Jerome S. 1966. *Toward a theory of instruction*. Cambridge, MA: The Belknap Press of Harvard University.

Clark, Richard W. and Bruce P. Zimmer. 1989. Mentoring? Does it work? *Lifelong Learning*. 12.7: 26-28.

Cochrane, David R. 1974. Theological education by extension: What it can offer churches in North America. *Theological Education*. (Summer): 259-265.

Conn, Harvie M. 1984. *Eternal word and changing worlds: Theology, anthropology and mission in trialogue*. Grand Rapids, MI: Zondervan Publishing House.

Conn, Joyce and Isaac and Margaret Simbiri. 1978. *Christian family living*. Nairobi, Kenya. Evangel Publishing House.

Conner, David W. 1989. *Distance education: Why not?* Wheaton, IL:Access (Monograph No. 2).

Covell, Ralph R. and C. Peter Wagner. 1971. *An extension seminary primer*. Pasadena, CA: William Carey Library.

Crider, Don and Seth Msweli. 1974. *The shepherd and his work*. Kisumu, Kenya. Evangel Publishing House.

Cunningham, Phyllis M. 1983. Helping students extract meaning from experience. In *Helping adults learn how to learn*. Ed. Robert M. Smith. *New directions for continuing education*. San Francisco, CA: Jossey-Bass Publishers. 19 (September): 57-68.

Dewey, John. 1937. *Experience and education*. New York, NY: McMillan, Inc.

Dominy, Peter. 1974. *Looking at the Old Testament, part I*. Kisumu, Kenya. Evangel Publishing House.

Draper, James A. 1989. Extending the network and content of Adult Education workers. *Convergence*. 22.2-3: 81-92.

Emery, James H. 1969a. The preparation of leaders in a Ladino-Indian church. *Theological education by extension*. Ed. Ralph D. Winter. Pasadena, CA: William Carey Library.

_____. 1969b. The Presbyterian Seminary in Guatemala three years later. In *Theological education by extension*. Ed. Ralph D. Winter. Pasadena, CA: William Carey Library.

_____. 1990. Accreditation and theological education. *Ministerial Formation*. 51 (October): 2-17.

Engel, James F. 1989. *Strategic planning for extension education*. Wheaton, IL: Access (Monograph No. 1).

Erikson, Edwin. 1989. Theological education by extension as education for extension. *Global Church Growth*. 25 (October-December): 8-9.

Esterline, David V. 1986. A proposal for the evaluation of theological education by extension. Ph.D. dissertation, Graduate Theological Union. Berkeley, CA.

_____. 1990. Community-based evaluation. *Ministerial Formation*. 51 (October): 18-26.

Fehr, Julie. 1983. ETD-Gabon after three years of operation. A profile of students: January 1980 to January 1983. Libreville, Gabon.

_____. 1989. Theological education and the local church. A report to the All Africa Conference. 24-28 April. Yamoussoukro, Cote d'Ivoire.

Ferris, Robert W. 1978. Defining TEE—issues and commitments. An unpublished paper.

_____. 1979. Structural dissonances inherent in traditional patterns of theological education. An unpublished paper.

_____. 1980. Curriculum guidelines for TEE. An unpublished paper.

_____. 1981. Overcoming problems in introducing change. Unpublished paper. 12-13 February. Taytay, Rizal, Philippines: PAFTEE Workshop.

_____. 1982. Philosophy and structure of accreditation: Theological education standards today and tomorrow. *Evangelical Review of Theology*. 6.2 (October): 299-314.

_____. 1984. The future of theological education. In *Cyprus: TEE come of age*. Ed. Robert L. Youngblood. Torquay, GB: Paternoster Press.

_____. 1985a. TEE consultation reviews, developments and challenges in Asia. *Theological News Incorporating Theological Education Today*. 17.3 (July-September): 1-3.

_____. 1985b. The role of Bible schools in preparing servant leaders. *Theological News Incorporating Theological Education Today*. 17.1 (January-March): 1-8.

_____. 1986. Accrediting TEE: Steps toward understanding and practice. *Theological News Incorporating Theological Education Today*. (October-December): 1-10.

_____. 1987. Linking formal and nonformal education. *Theological News Incorporating Theological Education Today*. (July-September): 1-9.

_____. 1990. *Renewal in theological education: Strategies for change*. Wheaton, IL: Billy Graham Center, Wheaton College.

Fischer, Joan Keller and Jane I. Evanson. 1979. Test scores don't tell the whole story. In *New directions for continuing education*. Alan B. Knox, Ed. San Francisco, CA: Jossey-Bass Publishers. 3: 29-36.

Foxall, George. 1990. ACTEA Directory of Theological Education by Extension Programmes in Africa. Published by the Accrediting Council for Theological Education in Africa, a ministry of the AEAM Theological and Christian Education Commission (TCEC). Kaduna, Nigeria.

_____. 1991. Profile of theological education by extension in Africa. An unpublished paper. 3-8 June. Jos, Nigeria: Second ACTEA All Africa Consultation.

Freire, Paulo. 1990a. *Education for critical consciousness*. New York, NY: Continuum Publishing Company.

_____. 1990b. *Pedagogy of the oppressed*. New York, NY: Continuum Publishing Company.

Gagne, Robert. 1965. *Conditions of learning*. New York, NY: Holt, Rinehart Winston. Third edition.

Garrison, D. R. and D. Shale. 1987. Mapping the boundaries of distance education: Problems in defining the field. *The American Journal of Distance Education*. 1.1: 7-13.

Gatimu, Kiranga. 1983. Emergence of nonformal theological education in Africa. *Theological News Incorporating Theological Education Today*. 15.2 (June): 5-8.

_____. 1985. Facing up to the challenge of training TEE workers in Eastern Africa today. *Theological News Incorporating Theological Education Today.* 17.2 (April-June): 1-4.

Gerber, Vergil, ed. 1980. *Discipling through TEE: A fresh approach to theological education in the 1980's.* Chicago, IL: Moody Press.

Groome, Thomas H. 1980. *Christian religious education: Sharing our story and vision.* San Francisco, CA: Harper and Row Publishers.

Gustafson, A. M. 1969. A Lutheran Theological Seminary for Bolivia. In *Theological education by extension.* Ed. Ralph D. Winter. Pasadena, CA: William Carey Library.

Hall, Darl Marideth. 1961. *The dynamics of group discussion: A handbook for discussion leaders.* Danville, IL: The Interstate Printers and Publishing, Inc.

Harrison, Patricia. 1977. Evaluation TEE: A theological Cinderella? *Asia Perspective No.7.* Asia Theological Association. 1-16.

_____. 1990. Evaluating TEE with special reference to the Pacific area. *Ministerial Formation.* 51 (October): 27-35.

Harshman, Carl I. 1979. The impact of the non-traditional degree: A case study. In *Assessing the impact of continuing education.* Ed. Alan B. Knox. *New directions for continuing education.* San Francisco, CA: Jossey-Bass Publishers. 3: 55-61.

Hill, Bradley. 1988. The fall and rise of TEE in one African church. *Evangelical Missions Quarterly.* 24.1 (January): 42-47.

Hill, Leslie D. 1974. *Designing a theological education by extension program: A Philippine case study.* Pasadena, CA: William Carey Library.

Hill, William Fawcett. 1977. *Learning thru discussion: Guide for leaders and members of discussion groups.* Beverly Hills, CA: Sage Publications Inc.

Hirst, Lester. 1986. Making TEE serve the needs of the churches. *Evangelical Missions Quarterly.* 22.4 (October): 420-424.

Hjelmefiord, Olaf. 1989. TEE, the key to the Bible. An unpublished handout prepared for TEE workshops. Middleburg, South Africa: Phumelela Bible School Extension, Alliance Church.

Hogarth, Jonathan, Kiranga Gatimu and David Barrett. 1983. *Theological education in context: 100 extension programmes in contemporary Africa.* Nairobi, Kenya: Usima Press.

Holland, Fred. 1970. Letter to Ray Buker, June. Wheaton College, Wheaton, IL: Billy Graham Center Archives (10-3).

_____. 1975. *Teaching through TEE.* Nairobi, Kenya: Evangel Publishing House.

_____. 1978. Theological education in context and change: The influence of leadership training and anthropology on ministry for church growth. D. Missiology dissertation, Fuller Theological Seminary. Pasadena, CA.

_____. 1980. For ministers only: Training *for* and *in* ministry. In *Discipling through theological education by extension.* Ed. Vergil Gerber. Chicago, IL: Moody Press.

_____. 1982. Contextualization and theological education: The who, how, where and what of ministry training. *Perception.* AEAM publication. 21 (December): 1-8.

_____. 1983. TEXT-Africa: Programming for ministry through theological education by extension. In *Ministry by the people: Theological education by extension.* Ed. F. Ross Kinsler. Maryknoll, NY: Orbis Books.

_____. 1991. Interview with the author.

Holmberg, Borje. 1979. Practice in distance education: A conceptual framework. *Canadian Journal of University Continuing Education.* 1.1 (Summer): 18-30.

Hopewell, James F. 1969. Preparing the candidate for mission. In *Theological education by extension.* Ed. Ralph D. Winter. Pasadena, CA: William Carey Library.

Hughes, Kate. 1990. Establishing a theological education by extension programme in Southern Africa: An evaluation of the first ten years. An unpublished paper. Johannesburg, South Africa: Theological Education by Extension College.

Illich, Ivan. 1971. *Deschooling society.* New York, NY: Harper and Row Publishers, Inc.

Joyce, Bruce and Marsha Weil. 1986. *Models of teaching.* Third edition. Englewood Cliffs, NJ: Prentice-Hall, Inc.

Kaye, Anthony R. 1985. Distance education. In *International encyclopedia of education*. Eds. Torsten Husen and T. Neville Postlethwaite. Vol. 3. Oxford, NY: Pergammon Press.

Kaye, Anthony and Greville Rumble. 1981. Origins and structures. In *Distance teaching for higher and adult education*. Eds. Anthony Kaye and Greville Rumble. London, GB: Croom Helm.

Keikung, Anjo L. 1985. Principles of andragogy as developed by Malcolm S. Knowles and their implications in theological education by extension in an Indian context. M. A. thesis, Trinity Evangelical Divinity School. Deerfield, IL.

_____. 1986. Theological education by extension in India. D. Missiological dissertation, Trinity Evangelical Divinity School. Deerfield, IL.

Khumalo, Alpheus, Ephraim Moalusi, and Stewart Snook. 1973. *New Testament survey, part one*. Kisumu, Kenya: Evangel Publishing House.

Kidd, J. Roby. 1973. *How adults learn*. Revised. New York, NY: Association Press.

_____. 1979. A nation of learners. *Convergence*. 12.1-2: 25-39.

Kinsler, Ross F. 1981. *The extension movement in theological education: A call to the renewal of the ministry*. Revised. Pasadena, CA: William Carey Library.

_____. Ed. 1983. *Ministry by the people: Theological education by extension*. Maryknoll, NY: Orbis Books.

_____. 1983. Theological education by extension: Equipping God's people for ministry. In *Ministry by the people: Theological education by extension*. Ed. F. Ross Kinsler. Maryknoll, NY: Orbis Books.

Kleis, Russell. 1974. *Program of studies in non-formal education. Study team reports of case studies in non-formal education*. East Lansing, MI: Michigan State University.

Knowles, Malcolm S. 1973. *The adult learner: A neglected species*. Houston, TX: Gulf Publishing Company.

_____. 1975. *Self-directed learning: A guide for learners and teachers*. Chicago, IL: Association Press, Follett Publishing Company.

_____. 1980. *The modern practice of adult education: From pedagogy to andragogy*. Chicago, IL: Follett Publishing Company.

Knowles, Malcolm S. and Associates. 1984. *Andragogy in action.* San Francisco, CA: Jossey-Bass Publishers.

Knox, Alan B. 1979a. Administrators. In *Enhancing proficiencies of continuing educators.* Ed. Alan B. Knox. *New directions for continuing education.* San Francisco, CA: Jossey-Bass Publishers.

_____. 1979b. What difference does it make? In *Assessing the impact of continuing education.* Ed. Alan B. Knox. *New directions for continuing education.* San Francisco, CA: Jossey-Bass Publishers. 3: 1-28.

Kolb, David A. 1984. *Experiential learning: Experience as the source of learning and development.* Englewood Cliffs, NJ: Prentice-Hall, Inc.

Kornfield, William J. 1976. The challenge to make extension education culturally relevant. *Evangelical Missions Quarterly.* 12.1 (January): 13-22.

MacKenzie, N., R. Postgate and John Scupham. 1975. *Open learning: Systems and problems in post-secondary education.* Paris, France: Unesco Press.

McKinney, Lois. 1973. Cultural attunement of programmed instruction: Individualized-group and expository-discovery dimensions. Ph.D. dissertation, Michigan State University. Lansing, MI.

_____. 1975. *Writing for theological education by extension.* A training course of 56 modules for writers of programmed instruction for TEE. Pasadena, CA: William Carey Library.

_____. 1981. Residence programs and TEE: A critical appraisal and a plan for renewal. *Theological Education Today.* 11.4 (December): 12-16.

_____. 1984a. Contextualizing instruction: Contributions to missiology from the field of education. *Missiology: An International Review.* 12.3: 311-326.

_____. 1984b. How shall we cooperate internationally in theological education by extension? In *Cyprus: TEE come of age.* Ed. R. L. Youngblood. Exeter, GB: Paternoster Press on behalf of WEF, ICAA.

_____. 1991. Interview with the author.

Mehta, Prayag. 1978. Dynamics of adult learning and development. *Convergence.* 11.3-4: 36-43.

Mezirow, Jack. 1972. Educating adults in family planning. *World Education Issues.* New York, NY: World Education. 1.

Moalusi, Ephraim, Stewart Snook, and Richard Jordahl. 1977. *New Testament survey, part two: Romans to 2 Thessalonians*. Kisumu, Kenya: Evangel Publishing House.

Mouton, Jane Srygley and Robert R. Blake. 1984. *Synergy: A new strategy for education, training and development*. San Francisco, CA: Jossey-Bass Publishers.

Moyo, Jonah and Grace Holland. 1973. *Bringing people to Jesus*. Kisumu, Kenya: Evangel Publishing House.

Mulholland, Kenneth B. 1976. *Adventures in training the ministry: A Honduran case study in TEE*. Nutley, NJ: Presbyterian and Reformed Press.

_____. 1984. TEE come of age: A candid assessment after two decades. In *Cyprus: TEE come of age*. Ed. Robert L. Youngblood. Exeter, GB: Paternoster Press for WEF and ICAA.

Nkosi, Moses. 1990. Interview with the author.

Patterson, George. 1974. Multiply churches through extension chains. *Church Growth Bulletin*. (July): 375-382.

_____. 1976. *Obedience oriented education*. Pasadena, CA: William Carey Library.

_____. 1981. The spontaneous multiplication of churches. In *Perspectives on the world Christian movement: A reader*. Eds. Ralph D. Winter and Steven C. Hawthorne. Pasadena, CA: William Carey Library.

_____. 1983. Extension Bible Institute (Northern Honduras): Theological education and evangelism by extension. In *Ministry by the people: Theological education by extension*. Ed. F. Ross Kinsler. Maryknoll, NY: Orbis Books.

Plueddemann, James and Carol Plueddemann. 1990. *Pilgrims in progress*. Wheaton, IL: Harold Shaw Publishers.

Pochi, Rev. Dan Chinai. 1990a. Interview with author.

_____. 1990b. Theological education by extension in Nigeria. M.A. research project. University of Jos. Plateau State, Nigeria.

Preiswerk, Matias. 1987. Popular education and popular theological education: Toward a definition of their spheres. *Ministerial Formation*. 37 (March): 5-21.

Prosser, Roy. 1967. *Adult education for developing countries.* Nairobi, Kenya: East African Publishing House.

Pulse. 1991. TEE time. Evangelical Missions Information Service. 26.19 (October): 1.

Recommendations. 1991. Summary of ad hoc committees recommendations for the future development of TEE in Africa. 3-8 June. Jos, Nigeria: Second ACTEA All Africa TEE Consultation.

Reed, Jeff. 1988. Church-based leadership training: A proposal. *Words of Fellowship.* 1.1 (Fall): 97-107.

Report. 1991. An unpublished paper on missionary departures from BEE work prepared for the African Inland Church: Biblical Education by Extension. April. Nairobi, Kenya.

Rosenblum, Sandra H. 1985. The adults role in educational planning. In *Involving adults in the educational process.* Ed. Sandra H. Rosenblum. *New directions for continuing education.* San Francisco, CA: Jossey-Bass Publishers. 26 (June): 13-25.

Rowen, Samuel F. 1967. *The resident-extension seminary: A seminary program for the Dominican Republic.* Miami, FL: West Indies Mission.

Sales, Richard W. 1976. Tripping and training in Botswana: The positive values of ministerial preparation by extension. *Christian Century.* (February): 116-120.

_____. 1977. Two or three and God: Extension theology recognizes that the teacher of the things of God is God. *Christian Century.* (February): 110-113.

Selfridge, Jack. 1974. *Following Jesus.* Kisumu, Kenya: Evangel Publishing House.

Sewart, David, Desmond Keegan and Borje Holmberg. Eds. 1983. *Distance education: International perspectives.* New York, NY: St. Martin's Press.

Skosana, James. 1991. Interview with author.

Snook, Stewart. 1986. *The Letter to the Hebrews* with the collaboration of Pogisho Pooe and Eunice Snook. Kisumu, Kenya: Evangel Publishing House.

_____. 1977a. A short history of the development of TEE and PI in South Africa. Unpublished paper for Training the Ministry. Pasadena, CA: Fuller Theological Seminary.

_____. 1977b. Theological education in South Africa among the Sotho and Zulu peoples. An unpublished paper for Training the Ministry. Pasadena, CA: Fuller Theological Seminary.

_____. 1980. Theological education by extension: What it *can* do; what it *cannot* do. An unpublished paper. Johannesburg, South Africa.

Sprunger, Frederic W. 1981. *TEE in Japan: A realistic vision.* Pasadena, CA: William Carey Library.

Srinivasan, Lyra. 1977. *Perspectives on nonformal adult learning.* New York, NY: World Education.

Stake, Robert E. 1967. The countenance of educational evaluations. *Teacher's College Record.* 687 (April): 523-540.

Summary. 1990. The Programme "Certificate of Biblical Studies." An unpublished paper for the African Inland Church. April. Nairobi, Kenya: BEE.

Thornton, Margaret. 1990. *Training TEE leaders: A course guide.* Nairobi, Kenya: Evangel Publishing House.

Turley, Phillip. 1989. An outline for changes to the teacher training course. An unpublished report. November. Nairobi, Kenya: AIC-BEE.

_____. 1990. BEE: Sweet as honey. *Today in Africa.* 189 (May-June): 18-19.

_____. 1991a. Extending the fence: Suggestions for the future of TEE in Africa. *Africa Journal of Evangelical Theology.* 10.1: 39-52. Adapted from a paper presented at the Second ACTEA All Africa TEE Consultation. 3-8 June. Jos, Nigeria.

_____. 1991b. Financial report for October 1, 1989 to September 30, 1990 and October 1, 1990 to March 31, 1991. March. Nairobi, Kenya: AIC-BEE.

Urbanization and TEE in Kenya. 1990. A questionnaire cross-tabulation by urban/rural location. Interim draft report prepared by the Urban Ministries Support Group with assistance from Mrs. Marsha Navamanie, Daystar University College and Rev. Phillip Turley, AIC-BEE. 10 November. Nairobi, Kenya.

Viertel, Weldon E. 1979. *A guide to decentralized theological education.* El Paso, TX: CARIB Baptist Publications.

Wagner, C. Peter. 1969. The Crises in ministerial training in younger churches. In *Theological education by extension.* Ed. Ralph D. Winter. Pasadena, CA: William Carey Library.

Walker, Louise J. 1969. The preparation of the materials. In *Theological education by extension.* Ed. Ralph D. Winter. Pasadena, CA: William Carey Library.

Ward, Ted. 1973. *The why and how of evaluation in nonformal education.* East Lansing, MI: Institute for International Studies for Education.

_____. 1974. Theological education by extension: Much more than a fad. *Theological Education.* (Summer): 246–258.

_____. 1977. Types of TEE. *Evangelical Missions Quarterly.* 13.2 (April): 79–85.

Ward, Ted and John Dettoni. 1973. Non-formal education: problems and promises. In *Non-formal education discussion papers.* Lansing, MI: Michigan State University.

Ward, Ted and Samuel F. Rowen. 1972. The significance of the extension seminary. *Evangelical Missions Quarterly.* 9.1 (Fall): 17– 27.

Ward, Ted and Margaret Ward. 1970. *Programmed instruction for theological education by extension.* Wheaton, IL: CAMEO.

Way, Kano Musuro. 1985. The plan of action as it applies to theological education by extension. An unpublished paper. Nairobi, Kenya: Daystar University College.

Wedemeyer, Charles. 1981. *Learning at the back door: Reflections on non-traditional learning in the lifespan.* Madison, WI: University of Wisconsin Press.

Weld, Wayne C. 1973. *The world directory of theological education by extension.* Pasadena, CA: William Carey Library.

_____. 1976. *Supplement to the world directory of theological education by extension.* Pasadena, CA: William Carey Library.

_____. 1980. *Supplement to the world directory of theological education by extension.* Wheaton, IL: CAMEO.

Winter, Ralph D. Ed. 1969. *Theological education by extension*. Pasadena, CA: William Carey Library.

_____. 1978. Class notes. Training the ministry. Fuller Theological Seminary. Pasadena, CA.

Young, Michael. 1978. Distance learning for adults: Some questions, issues and choices. *Convergence*. 11. 3-4: 72-81.

Young, Michael, et al. 1980. *Distance teaching for the third world: The lion and the clockwork mouse*. London, GB: Routledge & Kegan Paul.

Zigerell, James. 1984. *Distance education: An information age approach to adult education*. Columbus, OH: ERIC Clearinghouse on Adult, Career, and Vocational Education.

About the Author

Stewart George Snook is the field chairman for The Evangelical Alliance Mission (TEAM) in South Africa. After completing studies at Philadelphia Bible Institute, he earned a B.A. in history and an M.A. in Theology at Wheaton College. Stewart completed a second M.A., in missiology, from the Fuller Theological Seminary School of Missions in 1978 and recently was awarded the Doctor of Missiology degree from Trinity Evangelical Divinity School in Deerfield, IL.

Stewart Snook has held pastorates in New Jersey and Pennsylvania. In 1963, he and his wife, Eunice, accepted a missionary assignment to South Africa under TEAM. He was teacher, then principal, at the Evangelical Bible Institute in Rustenburg in the Transvaal. In 1974, he was appointed Director of Theological Education by Extension (TEE) by the TEAM South African field and then became chairman of that field in 1985.

Holding deeply felt convictions about each Christian believer's role in the world mission of the church, Stew Snook's life goals aim at training lay leaders for ministry and giving them a firm foundation in the Word of God. He believes TEE has proven useful in this regard in many situations where churches grow faster than they can produce leadership or where local church leaders cannot attend resident schools.

Stewart was the sixth missionary scholar in residence at the Billy Graham Center. He has written numerous papers on theological education and coauthored a series of books on the New Testament. These programmed texts have been translated into many of the languages of Africa, Alaska, and South America, and into some native American tongues.

Eunice Snook is also a Wheaton graduate. Vitally involved in the ministry in South Africa, Eunice has taught in a Bible College, led women's Bible studies, participated in TEE classes, typed many manuscripts—and as wife of the field chairman, she is responsible for the hospitality of the guesthouse.

Stewart and Eunice have two children. Son Steven holds a Ph.D. degree and does counseling as a psychologist with OASIS (Occupational Assessment Services for Industrial Systems) in Atlanta, Georgia. Daughter Carol serves with her husband at TransWorld Radio in Swaziland.